THE BEGINNER'S GUIDE TO COPYWRITING MASTERY HANDBOOK

LEARN THE SECRETS TO SELL ANYTHING TO ANYONE

LAWRENCE GIBSON

CONTENTS

Introduction   v

What Is Exactly Copywriting?   1
Believing In Your Company's Products   5
Create Your Product Description   8
Understand Your Customers   14
Persuasion Techniques – Liking, Consistency, Social Proof,   19
And More.
Principle Of Copy Writing   24
Write Attention-Grabbing Headlines And Opening   30
Tell A Story   35
The Power Of Bullet Points   44
Write A Killer Call To Action   50
Psychologically Advanced Copywriting Tricks   53
Essential Copywriting Techniques To Use Daily   73
Easy Copywriting Formulas That Convert   79
The Secrets To Copywriting Success   88
Important Questions To Ask Before You Hire A   92
Copywriter
Conclusion   97

INTRODUCTION

The power of words can change a company's future. This might be a strong claim, but after reading this guide, you will understand the reason for this statement. It is the use of effective copywriting techniques that offer value to customers.

Based on experience, this writer asserts that having a love for words is crucial to copywriting. Continuing education and experience can play their part, but when it comes to copywriting, it would not be possible to satisfy a client without it.

Start right away by telling yourself that in order to create value with words, you need to use effective copywriting techniques. These are full of a talking and connected language in which, along with the application of an SEO strategy, you get carried away by the rhythm of the sentences, the light and non-resonant sounds, breathing between commas and periods, all capable of giving effect to a thought.

The skill of mixing all these elements together is not easy to acquire at all. Writing may be for everyone but doing it to achieve a goal is one of the most difficult aspects of the big and complex world of content marketing. Many vital ingredients need to be present to achieve results through copywriting techniques:

- choose a strategy suited to the target
- evaluate the right tools to communicate
- organize useful resources for what is told
- consider the client as a person, and not as a public

To all these components, add the most important: the ability to tell by revealing one's own character. Only a company that offers its client something of himself can be appreciated. The customer wants to feel pampered and not deceived by the phrases made (what do you think when you read "industry leader"?). He wants to find out who is behind a brand, to feel part of something beautiful, because it is clean from logic oriented exclusively to the business. Further, the customer wants to bring stories home. It is not because he loves storytelling. Most often than not, he might not be even aware of what it is. He wants to know the stories because they transform a product or a service into something useful and indispensable.

Presenting a company with copywriting techniques

It is clear that in order to make a company known, it is necessary to choose the right words – words that talk about the business not with the objective of selling but offering added value instead. To accomplish this effectively, copywriting techniques are a big help. These are the tricks that word professionals use to mix strategy and heart together.

How do you do it concretely?

Before the indispensable techniques to show the corporate soul of a brand will be explained, there is something you must do beforehand.

Approach the screen.

Do not worry, you will only be told to scan each syllable well.

Before writing about a company, listen to what the entrepreneur has to say.

Do not think about the right words. For now, lay aside the thought that you need to put into practice everything you have learned about SEO copywriting. Forget the company's strategies for a moment. Take some time to listen to what the brand wants to tell you.

Translate his message and read what is inside his entrepreneurial heart. Live with the entrepreneur the emotions, and the features that make what he sells unique.

Listen to it several times, take a long breath and put everything in your mind.

Here and now, you are ready to write using copywriting techniques. Now, you can choose the right words. Five essential techniques are suggested:

1.Define a tone of voice that will speak for the company.

2.Capture your attention with an appealing incipit that contains the main keyword of your SEO strategy.

3.It takes care of the simplification and the legibility of the text.

4.Create a link with the reader through words.

5.Share a true story.

The copywriting explained to the client is how important it is to tell oneself online. If you follow this path, it becomes the best way to empathize with the customer who does not need a showcase site that displays a list of products and services. He wants to know and satisfy all his consumer curiosity, to understand, and imagine with his mind. All these are possible, thanks to words.

Company and reader become two characters of a common journey, in which one esteems the other.

A company or an entrepreneur who is presenting and offering himself online should do so without fear and doubt. He must not be afraid of making mistakes. In the event this happens, he admits the mistake and prepares to make improvements. A company grows in small steps together with the words it publishes. It does not insist on being seen for what it is not. It does not self-criticize, nor does it promise the impossible. In addition, it listens to the advice of those who follow its adventures on the web, those who show themselves to be human. If all these are allowed to happen, between a web marketing strategy and an essential dose of empathy with the customer, words can create value and lead to a result. This is how the fate of a company will change.

WHAT IS EXACTLY COPYWRITING?

What exactly is copywriting? Make a guess. Now, with your guess still fresh in your mind, let me give you a true glimpse of what copywriting is.

Copywriting is the aspect of writing copies for the sole purpose of marketing or advertising. The written copy is a piece of document meant to persuade a potential buyer or customer to buy the product or influence how they view the product in question differently.

In broadcasting, marketing, and advertising, someone who writes copies is called a copywriter or continuity (in broadcasting). The work of a copywriter is straightforward: create taglines, webpage content, and direct mail pieces. Copywriters who write web content prefer the name content writer to copywriters.

The scope of responsibilities a copywriter holds in his or her cap is not limited to the above list; it goes further than that. Copywriters also create newsletters, online ads, internet content, press releases, catalogs, brochures, and other marketing materials, TV and radio commercial scripts and many more.

Additionally, a copywriter also has some role to play in book publishing. In this field, the copywriter is responsible for writing the jacket flap and flap copy with a compelling summary of the book. As I have indicated, technology space has expanded tremendously. Today, copywriters are also very prevalent in social media, social networking, and blog posts.

Before the advent of technology, and the freelancing craze, copywriters were (and still are), employees within organizations such as public relation firms, advertising agencies, book publishers, creative agencies, and advertising departments within organizations. This has changed to a certain degree with the rise of the internet.

Many copywriters are choosing to become independent. They are choosing to freelance for different clients and specialized copywriting agencies. In this type of setting, the copywriter has more 'string' to his or her writing because they are able to perform tasks such as editing, message consulting, SEO consulting, proofreading, design and layout etc.

As a copywriter, you will have to be a team player because often, copywriters work within the confines of a creative team. For example, if you work for an advertising agency, the organization may pair you with an art director. However, your main role is to create a verbally and textually compelling content derived from the copy provided by the client. In essence, the responsibility of a copywriter is to tell a story; a story that resonates with the reader, viewer, or potential customer.

I find it necessary to point out that there is little difference between a copywriter and a technical writer. The only difference between the two is that the work of a technical writer is simply to inform and not persuade. Here is a good comparison of the two parts of writing despite the fact that the careers of either often overlap. A content writer's work is to write a car ad to persuade a potential customer, while the work of a technical writer is to write about the operations of the car from reading the manual.

If you are wondering why you should bother learning the skill of copywriting, here are a few reasons.

As a copywriter, you get a chance to influence the masses by creating an ad or creative piece that remains on the mind of the viewer.

You get to work in the exciting field of advertising for TV and radio. In addition, you get to interact with some interesting people in the field of broadcasting.

Content writing is a creative venture. Therefore, if you love writing, you get to enjoy yourself while making a ton of money (yes, copywriting is a very profitable business concept).

Now that you have a better understanding of what copywriting is, let us look at five things every copywriter should know.

Copywriting: origins

The term copywriting dates back to the nineteenth century and is specifically related to the journalistic world.

In the editorial offices of the most authoritative newspapers, the figure of the copywriter dealt with drawing up announcements of all kinds.

Subsequently, the advertising media boom, first in print and then on radio and TV, totally changed the cards on the table.

In fact, copywriting work was increasingly associated with advertising.

Contributing as a protagonist to the creation of a successful advertising campaign, starting from the creation of slogans to promote the product, were the main work activities for the copywriter, before the advent of the web.

Then, the success of digital marketing has radically changed his duties. So much so that in addition to the professionals who still work in tandem with the art director, who specializes in graphics, there are more and more freelancers covering the multiple textual aspects of the content put online: think for example of the texts for social networks, to corporate blogs where product reviews need to be structured for SEO, so that they are attractive to the various search engines, so that Internet users can find the relevant information.

In short, at present copywriting is an integral part of internet communication.

Knowing how to communicate the message of a corporate brand, using the right words, the appropriate vocabulary and the specific SEO oriented writing technique are requirements that only a few possess.

This is why companies are increasingly looking for highly specialized figures in the world of the business writer.

And perhaps this research should be based on even more selective criteria, given that unfortunately in an increasingly more competitive market like today, many companies tend to rely on those who ask for lower compensation.

This is a huge mistake. There are those who write and those who write well. And to those who write well, merit must also be paid to the economy.

BELIEVING IN YOUR COMPANY'S PRODUCTS

It's not enough to see a bottle of shampoo and describe it. Advertising is much more subtle than that. The public demands more. If there are similar products on the market, you have to believe that your company's product is better. Not only must you believe it, you must also think of ways in which you can demonstrate it. Copywriting may be limited only to a few words on a television advertisement, a small brochure, or an advert, all of which is very limited in duration. Within a set space of time, you have to produce words people will remember. There are several ad campaigns where this is obvious. Although many adverts irritate the public to the point of turning down the volume, their message is so clear consumers buy into the product, believing it to be better than anything the competition could come up with.

Looking at some everyday examples of popular campaigns that have worked, Head 'N Shoulders is popular all over the world because their copywriters latched onto the fact their shampoo dealt with a problem no one talked about. Everyone else was talking about shine and color, thickness and softness, but no one was actually promoting the idea that dandruff had a cure. Those working on this ad campaign cleverly made a point of not only telling the public about this issue, but of showing them with advertisements that left an impression. You saw the scalp before and after. You learned about the new content of the shampoo and you also learned that compared to other shampoos, there isn't another with the same results.

That's a lot to learn from a two-minute spot on TV, but clever copywriting is what lies behind the best campaigns. A copywriter needs to see an original angle people feel comfortable with. A copywriter needs to believe in the product because that sincerity will show in the words. But it's more than that. They have to come up with ideas as to why one choice is better than another. It isn't enough anymore to have just the brand name of a product, although this helps, of course. Effective copywriting needs to make the consumer feel like they are getting superb value for their money.

In the past twenty years, we have seen great changes in copywriting. There have been televised scripts read by people who were unconvincing, cute animals were introduced into advertising, and even instances where copywriting was creative and amusing. Nowadays, advertising has to have something special that makes the consumer feel his or her needs are being catered to and he or she is being pampered. One of the best lines of copywriting in the last 15 years is the L'Oréal campaign where the key words were "Because you're worth it."

The message you need to get across in copywriting has to be that powerful. When you consider that catchphrase, it was clever because it was aimed toward women who may have thought purchasing expensive items for the sake of vanity should be lower on their priority. However, when people latched onto the catchphrase "Because I'm worth it," millions of women saw another side of the beauty product industry. They began to justify their purchases simply because they began to feel they were special and that the products were specifically made and tailored to their needs.

Believing in the product helps considerably because it gives the copywriter food for thought. Brevity is everything. If you are working on writing words that will appear on a billboard or an advertisement on the side of a bus, people only get a few moments to read it. Thus, lengthy explanations will be wasted. Copywriters produce advertising all around us. If you don't understand the message about the product or event being advertised, the copywriter didn't do a very good job.

As a copywriter, you must take the product, look at it, and consider the best way possible to present the product so the public will see it as advantageous. If you get it right, you will experience success. If you get it wrong, chances are your copywriting days will be short-lived.

Exercise in copyright

Pick up an object in your room and imagine you have to sell this object. Close your eyes and imagine words that would make the public know they need that product. Then, instead of using the obvious descriptive words you wrote down for the product, look into alternative adjectives and widen your vocabulary. It's not enough to say something is great. In fact, this may limit the type of market you are trying to impress. Your audience may be more tempted by words such as "innovative" or other adjectives that seem to fit the product. Think of Apple computers and the immediate words one may think of are "crisp" or "sharp." When you begin to think in this manner, it helps you more easily fit the adjectives to products.

CREATE YOUR PRODUCT DESCRIPTION

Structure makes product descriptions easier to read and easier to write. Having a clear plan will help your creative process, especially if you go on to write a lot of product descriptions for yourself or a client.

Using structure will prompt you to write in an organized way that you can replicate over and over again. Of course, there are always times when you will have to deviate from your preferred structures, especially when you are working from a client's brief. Remember, whilst you can advise your client or suggest a structure for your product description, some clients will already have a clear idea of how and what they want you to write, and you will have to work within their brief.

Suggested Structure

The following is a suggested structure that will get you off the touchline. You will find that you have a preferred method but be careful not to fall into the trap of writing all your product descriptions using exactly the same structure as repetition may lead to your customers becoming bored and will negatively affect your sales conversion rates.

Headline

Write a catchy headline that draws the customer's attention and intrigues them enough to read the rest of your copy.

Begin your Copy

Try one of these methods:

Suggest an action

Try our new...

Think about this...

Take a look at our...

When you try...

Ask a question

Do you want...

Is ___ causing you ___

Did you know that ...

Have you ever thought that ...?

Set a scene

Avoiding making a scene at the vets is easy when you...

On a cold winter's day, there's nothing better than...

Back to school after the holidays can be hectic, so why don't you...

Juxtapose your product with an idea

Summer sunshine may feel great on your skin, but...

Your cat may be important to you, but have you tried...

Features and Benefits

Describe your product using features to prove your benefits. Make sure your customer knows how unique your product is. You won't have room to list all the possible features and benefits, focus on your ideal customer and their needs, concerns and desires.

Example:

With a super-fast speed and high heat setting, our new hairdryer will enable you to dry your hair quicker than ever before meaning that you'll always arrive at those special dates on time and looking your very best.

Further Relate the Product to your Customer and add a Call to Action

Suggest further how your product relates to your customer's life, suggest accessories and situations that may complement it and refer to any scene set in the earlier part of the structure. Include your vital call to action.

For example:

So, when you're feeling the cold, make sure you have ___ and don't worry about ___ again. Just order ___ now.

___ is the perfect complement to your ___.so click HERE to get one straight away.

So, order now and make sure that you are ready for ___.

When you feel the need for excitement, pick up your ___ and a ___ and get ready for the ride of your life. Want to know more? Read on.

Call us now to order your ___ and never feel the cold again.

Remember, this is just a suggested way of planning your structure and one that can create many variations in your product description creation. As you become more experienced, you will find many different ways of approaching the plan of your structure. Structure is always important as it gives your imagination and creative powers a starting point.

Length

More and more people are turning to online product descriptions to research products, 61% according to a 2012 poll by global research company Ipsos and this has been increasing every year since.

So, what is the ideal word count for your product description? It's important to get it right.

There are no hard and fast rules and no matter what the ideal length is, you may be restricted or governed by the media where the product description will be published. You may also have to follow instructions from a client.

However, if your copy is too short you won't have enough words to do your product justice and adequately describe the features and benefits that are targeted towards your chosen audience. Product descriptions that don't contain enough details fail to provide the customer with enough information to make an informed buying decision, making them likely to look elsewhere. You will also miss out on search engine traffic as you won't have enough room to include key words and phrases.

On the other hand, if your product description is too long, you risk overloading the customer with information. No one wants to wade through a ton of copy to find the facts that they want. When deciding on the length your copy should be, choose only the key features and benefits that are targeted towards your particular customer group. Different types of customer may require more or less information.

Many marketing professionals suggest a word count of between 250 – 400 words as being ideal if you have the space, but there are many product descriptions far shorter than that which do the job very well. Another option is to use a short description but to provide a button to click to read more where you can include longer, more detailed copy. People buying higher priced items tend to want to read more about them.

AIDA

As advertising becomes cleverer and more competitive, each product description has to work harder to attract a potential customer's attention and make the sale. Even as all advertising is becoming more sophisticated, the basic principles behind writing good sales copy remain.

The acronym AIDA is a useful tool for ensuring that your product description grabs attention and moves the customer through to converting to a sale.

The acronym stands for:

Attention

Interest

Desire

Action

Attention

You need to act quickly and grab your customer's attention. You can do this by writing a compelling headline for your copy. Be direct, don't be so clever or obscure that the meaning isn't apparent and make sure your headline is snappy and unique.

Interest

So, you've grabbed your customer's attention. Gaining their interest is perhaps the most challenging part of the AIDA model.

Engage your reader by quickly demonstrating the main benefits that the product will bring to them. Help them pick out the messages that are important to them by using small chunks of text, bullets and sub-headings – all these tools make your copy easier to read and more likely to hold the customer's interest.

Desire

The desire part of the AIDA model is closely related to the interest segment. You need to be able to convince your customer that they need your product. The clearest way of doing this is by appealing to your customer's needs, concerns and desires.

Action

Finally, be direct and tell your customer what you want them to do. Don't leave them interested but unsure of their following step: tell them what to do! This could be clicking to buy the product, phoning an order line, sending a mail order or visiting a particular website for further details.

UNDERSTAND YOUR CUSTOMERS

The second half of information that you need to get is information about your customers. By the way, some of you might think that knowing your customers should be done first before knowing your product. Yes, that is true. But it is also true that knowing your product should be done first, too. So, what exactly do you need to do? Nothing. Just do whatever you feel like doing first.

Knowing your product or knowing your customers can be done interchangeably. That means that you can do any of the two first. Usually, it really depends on your situation. And it is common that copywriters are often situated to know what the product is first and are restricted to a predefined target audience.

However, even if you already have a predefined target audience (usually set by your boss or client), you still need to know them. By knowing them further, you might find important data that you can exploit to improve your copy.

Also, be reminded that no copy can attract all customers. In most cases, you might need to use two different copies in order to achieve a higher lead acquisition rate.

With modern advertising platforms, like the one in Facebook, you can target your ads toward a defined set of people with ease. Due to that, it is common nowadays for clients, who use such ad platforms, to request multiple sets of copies.

Anyway, moving forward...

Know Your Customer Base

Before anything else, get to know the people who buy your products and/or services. Why not jump straight to the people who want to buy or will want to buy, or need to buy? The explanation is simple. Customers or converted leads are more profitable.

Making customers loyal is cheaper than getting new customers. Making a customer buy again is much easier because they have better understanding of your product and your company. And the most important point is that loyal customers are the most powerful marketing and advertising tool.

Ever heard of word-of-mouth advertising? Yes. Because of that, loyal customers must be always given attention—not to mention that they are double-edged swords. If you do not take care of them, they can easily become detractors. But that is going far off-topic.

What are the things you need to write down? For starters, start out with gender. Does the product sell well to males or females or both? The factors are age, occupation, legal status, and location. Depending on the product that you advertise, you might need more information or categories like those that are relevant to your product's sell ability.

For example, young single male adults (aged 18-35) in Bakersfield, California often buy the E-Bike 6000. Most of them are office workers.

Define Your Customer Base

Once you have a faint idea about your customer base, you will need to specify some details. You need to know them more to be precise. In this part, you might need to do some legwork.

Normally, the best way to get this information is through surveys or random interviews. What do you need to ask them? A lot of things. But mostly, you need to know their interests.

Knowing their interest alone can let you have great insights regarding your customer. This insight will allow you to write a copy that can suit their needs or wants. You can define the slant that will work on them.

For example, if most of your customers have interests in racing, you can write your copy using sports racing as an angle.

Know Why Your Customers Love Your Product

Aside from knowing your customers' interests, you must know why your customers buy or love your product. This essential piece of information is crucial in your copy and other marketing efforts of your company.

Knowing this information can help you have a better idea on the strengths and benefits of your product. Also, you will exactly know the problems that your product alleviates. Of course, knowing this and the interests of your customer can be exhausting and will require some of your company's resources.

However, if you are just a freelance copywriter, this can become a difficult task. Unless your boss or client provides you with the resources or will do the research themselves, expect that you will be forced to get these pieces of crucial information from your head.

Of course, do not be discouraged. Despite not having actual data, you can still make an almost accurate guess of what customers might be thinking. After all, you are just like them: a human being and a customer.

The only problem is that, if you hate the product, you will have a difficult time generating these ideas. So, before you take on job offers, be sure to be at least familiar and interested in the products or services that you are going to write copies for.

But wait. You can actually have a better guess even if you do not talk to the customers themselves. Thankfully, you can just use the Internet. Look for customer reviews about your product. Depending on the product you will advertise, you might not get sufficient data. You can also look at reviews from similar products if you get nothing from yours.

On the other hand, if the Internet fails you, try to ask your friends and family for any feedback on the product.

Know Your Potential Customer Base

Once you know who your customers are, the future step is to know the people that you want to buy your product. If you have a boss or client, he might have already set this part. On the other hand, if you are the one who needs to fill that detail, you might want to sell the product to almost everyone. But that will not do any good—for now.

At this point, you need to create the profile of the potential leads you want to attract. You cannot just settle for everybody. Remember that any copy cannot do that. So, what should you do? Settle for a small and defined demographic.

Since you have a defined customer base, all you need to do is to alter it a bit. For example, since males aged 18-35 buy the E-Bike 6000, females aged 18-35 might become attracted to the product as well.

On the other hand, the option to completely alter the initial customer base demographic is possible, too, as long as you have good reason, or you will create multiple copies. For example, you can try to cater to married adult females aged 36-50 in San Francisco, California. The reason is that an e-bike can help them alleviate the pain of using their cars, commuting, or walking when doing grocery shopping.

Targeting a completely different demographic is often discouraged. After all, if you are only set to creating one copy, you must always ensure that the copy will also click with your customer base.

After all, it is a bit impossible that you have already gotten all the people within your customer base demographic to buy your product. Do note that getting customers within a proven market is much easier than getting customers from unknown territory.

PERSUASION TECHNIQUES – LIKING, CONSISTENCY, SOCIAL PROOF, AND MORE.

Part of learning to be a successful copywriter is learning how to be more persuasive. To do this, it's necessary to dig into psychological ideas and understand what makes people tick, and how to motivate them to take action. Being persuasive isn't immoral or bad – it's part of everyday life and how we interact with people. Becoming more persuasive in your copywriting will be an eye-opener, a look into the world of salesmanship and, more generally, how to be persuasive in everyday life.

The power of rhyme.

Ideas that rhyme are more persuasive. For example, it's more persuasive to say, "This product is made from great grapes." Is more persuasive than "This product is made from amazing grapes." Of course, this doesn't mean you should be speaking poetically all the time. It does mean that sprinkling in rhymes at key moments of copy can be powerful.

The power of reciprocity.

A great way to persuade people to buy from you is to be the first in providing value. This is the principle that content marketing is based off. If you can first solve a small problem for someone, they are more likely to come to you later and pay you to solve a bigger problem. For example, they come to your website to learn how they can clean their car in half the time, they then come to your website to buy car insurance. You've solved a small problem, they feel that they need to reciprocate by paying you for something, so they buy car insurance.

The power of oddness.

Things that are bizarre and unusual are more compelling than something bland and ordinary. For example, the tagline "Our laptops are like spaceships for your mind," is more memorable than, "our laptops are fast and good for web browsing." Again, this doesn't mean everything needs to become ridiculous, but as an occasional tool to grab attention and be persuasive, it works.

The power of authority.

If someone in a position of authority publicly approves your product, the more likely others are to buy it. Ideally, this is someone who is a leader in the field, has qualifications, and a great reputation – all of these things will make their opinion more powerful. When you show this person likes your product, your copywriting becomes more persuasive to the customer.

The power of your peers.

As well as people in positions of power, people are largely affected by what people in a similar position to them are doing. The most powerful example of this is when all your friends are doing something, you want to do that thing as well. Practically, you don't know what the friends of the reader are doing, but you can address people in their demographic. For example, if you know most of your clients are 20-25, you can say "20-25-year-olds love our products," then readers in that age range will think "I'm in that demographic, maybe I'll like it too." This is the power of belonging and group identity. Use it mindfully and your copy will be more persuasive.

Take responsibility for negative experiences

It might seem counter-intuitive but being able to take responsibility and own up to a failure will actually make you and/or your business more compelling. Of course, you don't want to create a reputation for being incompetent. But occasionally taking complete responsibility and being able to say "sorry" correctly will help your business to be more persuasive because it is better perceived.

Share learning experiences with your audience

This is similar to the preceding point. Creating a public image of a business that is human and humble will make it more appealing. People don't want to buy from a brand that seems to always be perfect because they know the real world is messy and no one or thing is perfect. A business that takes responsibility, apologizes when appropriate, and makes its learning experiences public is better perceived by its clientele.

Be specific with promises.

When selling a product or service, it helps to be very specific in the promises you make. For example, it is better to say, "Lose 6 pounds of fat in 6 weeks with our product" than it is to say, "Lose fat with our product." Specific promises are easier to grasp for the customer and they'll feel more confident in the product. Grey, fuzzy promises are less appealing. Make promises as specific as possible, and also make downsides as specific as possible. For example, minimize the downside by saying "there is a 30-day money back guarantee" rather than "we have an excellent returns policy." The former gives a clear, definite promise to the customer that they can feel confident in, the latter is less appealing because the customer is more unsure what they are getting.

Get emotional.

People buy when they have their emotions stirred. You want the reader to feel excited by what the product will give them – you want them to feel the crushing downside if they don't get the benefits you are promising. Do everything you can to push the potential customer to feel strong emotions and push the upside hard whilst antagonizing the customer's fears.

Newness and novelty are powerful.

Differentiation in the marketplace is a powerful way to make your product seem better than the competition. If it's the first in the product, that's fantastic. If it isn't the first, make it different, better in some definitive way. Always think about how you can present something as being better and newer. Also, don't be afraid to focus on the unusualness of the product.

Use testimonials.

This comes back to minimizing risk. No customer wants to take a risk when they buy a product. So, the more you can ease all their worries, the better. To do this, have multiple, excellent testimonials throughout your marketing.

If in doubt, discount.

Emphasizing the cost savings of a product is always a great move. People love a deal. There is nothing new here. Consider the positioning of the product or service in the marketplace. If you have something more premium, perhaps make the price an afterthought. If the product or service is deliberately priced to be competitive, make this prominent in the sales material.

Sell time.

As well as cost savings, customers are trying to save time. Therefore, when positioning a product, focus on the ways in which it will save time for the customer. Everyone wants to save time – it's perhaps the most valuable commodity humans have. This means that you'll want to focus on how fast the product is to take effect, and how little time is needed to put it into place. Think "6-minute abs". In this example, "6 minutes" is such a small-time investment it makes the sale a lot easier.

We can all imagine finding 6 minutes a day to work out our abs – pushing this aspect of the product makes it highly desirable.

Start and end strong.

When you are listing a series of benefits to a customer, it is helpful to start and end with the best. This is so you get their attention initially and push their emotional state at the end, so they choose to buy. This applies to any form of sales text, whether it is an email, article, or landing page. There has to be a hook initially, and there has to be a clear, strong push at the end.

Test what works for your brand.

Every brand will have some persuasion techniques they currently rely on more than others. Take note of these and then begin to integrate new ones and add new creative directions for the sales copy. However, you don't want to be doing this in the dark. The best way to proceed with a campaign is to measure results and then double down on what is working. Do A/B testing whenever possible. This simply means trying one mode against another and then choosing the mode that sells more. For example, create two different sales emails to send to your email list. Have one focus more on time savings and the other focuses on cost savings. Send these emails out and then track which email has the best results. You now know which persuasion tactic is better suited to the brand and where to focus in future. Always be testing. Find what works. Do more of that.

PRINCIPLE OF COPY WRITING

Nice to work in the world of copywriting. You are a writer, but not a simple scribbler: move the masses with a title, increase the conversions of a project by changing the subject of the newsletter.

Of course, this is the shared idea. Everyone believes this is the world of the copywriter. And everyone sees this professional figure as a sort of sorcerer, a snake charmer, and a hypnotist. The copywriter uses words to exploit the dark psychological.

As often happens when creativity is involved, it is difficult to establish principles to guide work. However, we can outline:

It is essential to identify the target you want to reach: The message is effective only if it adopts a language suitable for the target audience, and the more specific it is, the easier it is to grasp. Also, the form of creativity must be adapted to the content of the brief, the objective is to sell, and the product must occupy a leading position with respect to the creative idea. Precisely for this reason, it is important to follow the principle of the Unique Selling Proposition (USP), or the formulation of a single creative idea, which will have to stress the product feature considered most important when designing the strategy. Besides, formal contradictions within the ad must be avoided, it is important, for example, that image and text say different things, not to overlap. A well-designed formal structure makes the ad easier to decode and allows you to get into tune more quickly with the target audience.

Apart from the fact that the world of persuasive copywriting is very well known, there are no obscure techniques; social proof, the principle of scarcity, benefits, use of numbers to communicate reliability. But they must be used decently.

You have to embrace the path with the principle of copywriting. That is writing that exploits the strengths, pointing towards the goal (conversions). But respecting the reader, the customer. You must respect the readers; do you agree? Perfect I guess you said yes, then let's go deeper into some points on principle of copywriting and writing for the people you love.

Testimonial

That is a testimony to confirm the quality of your product or service. The testimonials trigger the mechanism of social proof: to follow the mass and the opinions of those who make a public choice. Any advice to optimize testimonials:

- Use first and last name.

- Make the testimonial traceable (email, site).

- Choose a real image.

Above all, use a real, objective text without constraints. Usually, the testimonials are born thanks to a request, but you must never push towards testimonies that follow your criteria. Let the testimonial speak naturally: don't influence. And above all do not modify the text.

Numbers

Numbers are fundamental, especially when you use them to communicate reliability and precision. They work well with statistics; here is an example: 73% of Facebook users click on the links. The percentage communicates that there is a study at the base, scientific support. So reliable.

Using the numbers means knowing the numbers, telling the copy how they were collected and which year they refer to. But above all, what is the sample examined. To omit, for example, that 73% is aimed at American users in 2011 means taking the reader for a ride.

Headline

Here you play the reader's attention in social media and a good percentage of clicks. So, you have to work on a good headline. But above all on a fair, truthful headline, linked without compromise to the contents of the page.

The click baiting phenomenon has raised attention to a theme that has always characterized the web: authors use deceptive titles to bring people to the site and earn clicks. Do you know what this means? Rubbish. You have to work hard on the titles, you have to find the solution to attract the reader's attention, but your main objective is simple: to inform.

That is to give clear information on the subject that the reader will be able to deepen in the text. Some researches leave interesting data: one of the best solutions to combine clarity and effectiveness in a headline is the bulleted list. The numbers allow you to work on clarity, even if you can't just bet on this solution.

Scarcity

Only 10 places available, 24 hours are missing, and then you will no longer be able to access the discount. Scarcity is a psychological lever that bends the user: it lacks little, move, you can't wait. You must act immediately. Now. And to take advantage of the scarcity, you have to create real offers, without falling into the mattress syndrome.

We try every day to distinguish ourselves and to have access to what others do not have. Promotions that have a time limit, or a limited number, increase the impression that the product is of greater value.

But in addition to rarity, let us not forget secrecy and difficulty as factors to make a good more desirable.

That is the perennial offering. Do you remember the telesales of the mattresses? Every day was the day when you could take advantage of the maxi offer: buy a mattress and get an apartment. Pots, sheets, bicycles, televisions. Accurately outline the offer and do not concede too much; this is the advice.

Benefit

Benefits are fundamental to the work of the copywriter. Because they allow you to tell the potential customer the reasons to perform an action, to make a choice. In most cases the benefits are summarized in a bulleted list: you don't have to exaggerate; you have to insert the main reasons that should push users to choose your solution.

But above all, you must not boast false potential. In these cases, it is easy to want to aim high, but think: what will people think after discovering the flaw? Your goal is not to increase sales but to turn every customer into an evangelist. This way they will increase sales for you. And you can't do it if you lie to the people.

Reciprocity

Free trial periods, sample offers, access to confidential content, welcome coupons are all classic tools that respond to this psychological leverage: nobody likes to be in debt. It is an unpleasant feeling that we feel obliged to rebalance. If someone makes a concession, especially if unexpected, we feel obliged to reciprocate. For this reason, it is used to obtain a greater favor than the one granted, as well as when on the web we offer a discount or a free download in exchange for data that will serve us to better profile the user.

Commitment and Coherence

Having taken a commitment, our beliefs (and motivations in case someone asks us) align themselves consistently with that choice.

The voters feel closer and more certain to the party chosen immediately after the vote: no one would admit they were wrong. And so even when we rely on a brand: first of all, we are not defending that product, but our choice. This leverage is fundamental in social campaigns, where we must try to get the user to confirm their consent on different channels.

Getting Social

The more people share an idea, the more likely it is that it is valid, that is: without a reference model or specific knowledge acquired, the majority is followed yes exactly, it is the basis of collective indifference for which nobody moves a finger to help a person so many more people are around. Think of fake laughter or audience applause in TV studios. So, if a product page has good reviews, we will rely more on buying.

Sympathy

Sympathy and contrast are psychological levers well known to anthropology. Often it is sufficient to name the friend of the person to whom a product is sold to lead the negotiation to succeed. Factors that inspire sympathy are similarity, beauty, success, compliments, and in general, all positive associations but not always true.

As is known, beautiful and established testimonials have more potential in creating consensus and following.

Contrast

Any person who enters a real estate agent already knows that the first proposal will be the worst. To channel the buyer's decision towards the desired solution, it will be advisable to subject the person first to very demanding or exaggerated action, or one that is definitely to be discarded. However, subsequent proposals will be more favorable.

Authority

In the absence of a strong personal idea, authority is followed in the matter. We do it as children, and advertising with the various testimonials has always done so.

It is a lever of very ancient acquiescence, dormant in our animal unconscious, which in the evolution of society has been maintained over time. Think of the charm of the uniform, rather than that reassuring white coat used by actors who are perceived as a symbol of reliable scientific authority.

Hence, writing is love, and principles of copywriting are the concrete demonstration of this concept. The goal is important; the copywriter must give your company one more chance to increase conversions. But credibility is also important, not to mention respect for those who read your texts.

WRITE ATTENTION-GRABBING HEADLINES AND OPENING

Writing good copy takes practice and discipline, but it also takes something that makes many of us cringe: homework. To write compelling ad copy, you're going to have to look at the project from every angle. Who are you writing for? What do they want to read? What is going to grab their attention? What are the best keywords to include? Should you use a familiar, conversational tone, or is this audience strictly business? The successful copywriter knows the answers to these questions before he or she writes even a single word.

Of course, once the process has begun, every copywriting project should start the same way: with a headline. We can't stress how important the headline is - the success or failure of your copywriting services depend on your ability to craft a headline with a gravity well that could be measured by NASA. Hyperbolic as it may sound, if your reader doesn't make it past the headline, you don't have a reader.

The 3 responsibilities of a Headline

A Headline Should Announce Your Products' Biggest Benefit

Unless you attract the reader's attention right up front you can count on your visitors to stop reading in about 3 seconds or less. That's about all the time your headline has to make a difference. That is why your headline must grab the reader's attention by clearly stating the biggest benefit someone will get from reading the rest of your sales letter right away.

A Headline Should Be Powerful Enough to Make Them Want to Read More

Your headline should compel your prospect to keep reading the rest of your sales letter in your website. It is definitely important to make a powerful statement about your headline without giving away so much information that someone won't have to read the rest of the message to learn more.

A Headline Should Deliver an Entire Mini-Sales Message

If you think about it, you'll see that your headline is really a standalone sales message. It is designed to sell someone on wanting to read the body of the message. Readership studies show that 80% of your prospects will read only the headline before deciding whether or not they want to know more.

Secrete strategies to create a magnificent Headlines

Let's take a look at some of the secret strategies that you can use when copywriting to create a magnificent headline that will work like a magnet for your readers.

Size Matters!

It seems like we begin every copywriting guide with this tip, but it bears repeating. If your headline doesn't fit neatly into a Tweet with space for links and hashtags, it's not a successful headline. 90-120 characters is the sweet spot and remember that search engines only index the first 65 characters, so make sure that your headline begins with a bang.

Avoid Ambiguity.

Your reader should know what they're getting into before they click your article. If you've stumbled upon a masterful pun or bit of wordplay that may be clever and eye-catching but isn't so clear as to the content of your post, save it for the subhead or body text. Be clever and witty later - the headline is just the hook.

Who Else Wants It?

This is one secret that has been proven to work over and over again, and is one of the fundamental secrets of good headline crafting: use your headline to imply that your subject is already something that others know, use, enjoy, or are otherwise engaging in, and therefore that your reader is missing out on something important by not clicking. "Who Else Wants to Lose 10 Pounds?" Well, I certainly do!

Add a Little Mystery.

Use of words like "Secret" or "Little-Known Facts" will help draw readers in, as they will believe they're getting information that others aren't aware of. "Buying a House" isn't a compelling headline - but "The Secret to Getting the Best Mortgage Rate" or "Little-Known Facts about Getting Approved for a Home Loan," on the other hand, will draw in readers who are looking for insights they can't find anywhere else. Are you not convinced that it works? Look at the headline for this article one more time. Convinced yet?

Use Numbers.

Numbers help to quantify what you're talking about. "Getting a Better Body" is a fine headline, but "Getting a Better Body in 2 Weeks" is better, and "10 Steps to Get a Better Body in 2 Weeks" is better still. With numbers, particularly those 10 and below, readers feel like they know what they're getting into. An article on weight loss is still an article, and today's Internet reader is fickle and wants information in a hurry. 10 tips, on the other hand, sounds easy to scale and simple, and even the most-flighty reader can stick around for a list of 10 items. Second, adding the "in 2 weeks" to the end amplifies your claim and helps you stand out in a field of other articles about similar subjects.

The Speedy Approach.

As we've said, readers are fickle. Using the Internet to find answers and solve problems has become second nature to most of us. Websites offer quick answers to virtually any of our questions, from home improvement to healthcare, and good copywriting taps into this mindset. When you write a headline that fills the quick-fix, instant-gratification need, you're going to be honey for the speedy-bee reader. Items like "Get Rid of Carpenter Ants Once and for All" or "The Quickest Way to Get Over a Cold" are almost guaranteed to outperform articles with the same information with a blasé headline.

Amplify It.

So, you have a good hook and you've got a decent headline: "10 Ways to Get Rich." Not too bad, but there's some room to grow, and we can amp up your copywriting a bit with the use of some powerful adjectives and bold claims. If "10 Ways to Get Rich" is a decent headline, "10 Ways to Get Filthy Rich in Just One Year" is a fantastic one. Remember the other copywriting rules, though; keep it Tweetable, and don't make promises in your headline that you can't keep in your post.

Crafting Amazing Openings

The second most important part of the ad after headline is Opening paragraph.

You'll discover:

•Amazing way to grab attention and force him to keep reading. Plus Make your sales message more readable.

•Keep sentences as short as possible, without sacrificing the clarity or power of the message. Short sentences get read fast and easy. Long first sentences risk losing them. They can become boring.

•You should stick to the same principle as in headline. You must be sure the first paragraphs of you copy explode interest and curiosity.

Answer the question: Why I should read this?

In opening paragraph, you want to get your reader's attention to what comes after. You want to arouse so much curiosity in your prospect that he can't help but keep reading. You want to push the prospect forward throughout of your copy

In opening paragraphs, you elaborate problem that your prospect has. Also, you may give him announce why he should read your copy. Further, you appeal to the emotional pain of your prospect.

TELL A STORY

What is Storytelling?

Storytelling is a lot of different things. At its core, storytelling is the use of language and narrative in order to communicate something to an audience. The content of the story itself can be fictional (made up) or factual (using real events, people, and data). Stories themselves can serve multiple purposes as well, such as to explain an idea, deliver a message, or simply to be entertaining. Because stories can be quite flexible, let us take a look at what storytelling is and isn't so that we can narrow down the definition.

When it comes to our marketing, we want to ensure that there is useful or insightful information in our stories. This is because we ultimately want to use our stories to help drive our conversion rates. Another way of framing the idea of useful information is to say that our stories have a point. There is an idea or concept that they want to get across to the audience. For example, if you run a bakery, then you may want your point to be how delicious your cookies are. You could do this by just writing, "we have the most delicious cookies in town." But that isn't very catchy, is it? A more eye-catching way of doing the same thing would be to write a story about one of your customers, someone who goes out of their way to always visit your bakery when they are in the area, or who even makes special trips to get cookies from you despite living so far away. The point of the story is still that "we have the most delicious cookies in town," but now there is an intriguing story that makes us want to know more. Why is that?

Did you notice the main difference between the simple slogan and the story? It is that we added a character into the mix. Stories revolve around characters. Notice I didn't say people. There are many stories in which the characters are animals. For example, an animal shelter is much more likely to feature animals as their characters than people. Characters offer readers someone to see themselves reflected in and someone to connect to emotionally. When you are telling stories as a brand, you need to make sure that your characters are your customers. Since people identify with characters, making a character into a customer helps to make the reader feel like a customer as well.

Another core point of storytelling is the concept of narrative structure. A story begins, progresses to the middle, and then closes with an ending. The best stories offer some form of arc throughout, one in which the character changes. In the bakery example, our customer begins without cookies, travels to get to the shop, and ends with cookies. Tied to the customer getting the cookies is also an emotional element. The character started with a desire, worked to achieve that desire, and then was happy with the outcome. A story with a beginning, middle, and end follows what is called the three-act structure, and it is the most widely used story structure in existence. By following this structure and trying to incorporate an emotional experience into the structure, you create stories that can be followed by any and everyone.

Before we look at what a story is not, there are two important elements left to discuss that tie into storytelling as a brand rather than storytelling as a generalization. Your brand or business is made up of people and values. Storytelling is one of the ways that you can share the motivations and values of the brand and the people who run it. If you were running an organization that helped people fight for equal rights, you wouldn't share stories that showed somebody as being unequal in the end. You may share a story about how somebody was treated unequally, stood up for themselves, and was then treated equally because that shows the journey of achieving what you believe in. When brands share stories, they are also sharing their beliefs. They aren't just writing out a mission statement with their goal but connecting those beliefs with an emotional experience that sticks with readers long after they have finished reading.

Storytelling also isn't just sending out an advertisement for your merchandise. Now that so many people have stopped reading newspapers and watching television commercials, brands need to be smarter with their advertising. Rather than just telling someone they should buy your stuff; you now need to provide them value through your marketing. Since the most effective marketing is now done on social platforms, it is important to understand that people are choosing to come to your brand to see what they say. No one is forced to watch an advertisement as they had been in the past. Value is the key. There any many ways that we can provide people with value in our marketing, but we're focusing on storytelling. Storytelling provides an emotional experience, which is in and of itself, something of value. When that emotional experience is coupled with useful information, the value doubles, and people will love it.

It is important to remember the concept of structure in your storytelling. This means that you can't just write a couple of thousand words and put it out into the world and expect it to make a difference. You also don't want to simply show people something cool that happened. While cool things happening to your brand are great to share, sharing them in the form of a story will always lead to better results. It's the difference between telling someone that you graduated from university with honors, versus telling someone about how you grew up in a low-income family that couldn't even dream about sending you to college, which meant that you had to study extra hard to get to the top of your class so that you could secure a full-ride scholarship and make your parents prouder than they ever had been before. Adding context and narrative progression to those cool events turns a boring post into an inspiring story.

Why Do Marketers Tell Stories?

A few reasons have been mentioned above, but there are important ones that haven't come up in our discussion yet. There is a misconception in the general public that marketing is simply about telling people "buy our products." While this is the goal of marketing, those of us who do marketing know it is not even remotely close to how complex our approach to marketing is. There is a lot that goes into marketing, and it doesn't do just to hand a possible customer some numbers or copy. There are three core ideas that storytelling handles best for marketers.

The first is the way that stories help marketers to take abstract or complex concepts and make them easy to understand. Anyone who has studied a difficult subject knows that wrapping your head around a new idea isn't always easy. Stories are one way that we are able to grasp an idea more readily. An example of this in action in the classroom would be when a teacher turns a math problem into a story so that you understand the real-world application of the problem you are struggling with. Taking the abstract idea and turning it into a solid that we can grasp makes it easier to understand the way that everything connects with our experiences as human beings. An example of this in action is the way that Apple markets its gadgets. Instead of focusing on telling people how much processing power their computers have, they instead sell people on the things that they can do with their computers. The technical talk is still available for anyone interested in looking it up, but by sharing stories about what users have done on their computers, Apple has been able to boil a complex concept down to the way that real people have made use of them.

Stories also bring people together in a big way. We'll hear more about this in a moment because this goes back far into our evolutionary past.

The stories we experience in our modern day living express emotions and experiences which we all share. Being that we are all humans, we can understand what it is like to fall in love, or to be sad. We can understand the relief that comes with finally finding a product that provides us with what we were looking for and makes our lives easier. By connecting to stories, people feel more connected to each other. When your brand tells stories, this helps people to feel more connected to both your other customers and to the brand itself. Talk about a win-win situation!

Stories can also inspire and motivate people. When the animal shelter tells a story about the hardship that a particular dog has been through, this elicits an emotional response from the listener and makes them more likely to want to go out and adopt a dog themselves. When you share a story about how a customer travels out of their way to get your cookies, you motivate others to take the same action to see if they feel the same level of joy when they eat your cookies. Inspiration is actually a great selling tactic, yet there doesn't seem to be a lot of brands that have tapped into this particular strategy yet. Get ahead of the curve by considering how your stories can motivate.

Numbers and product descriptions don't inspire or bring people together. Hearing that your company's new vacuum has a suction power of 550 W doesn't help people to grasp its concept. But telling a story about how someone couldn't get the gunk out from between their floorboards until they tried your newest high-powered vacuum does. It makes it clear that this vacuum has enough power to get specific tasks done, it gives a character for the reader to connect with, and it inspires them to seek out a more effective product (your product) in their own lives.

Stories: A Neurological Overview

When we read a great story, a bunch of things happens inside our brains. One process which is triggered is mirroring. Say we're listening to a story out loud, the parts in our brains that would be trig-gering are very similar to those that trigger in the person who tells the story. Everyone who is around to listen will be more or less on the same wavelength psychologically. This helps to connect the person experiencing the story with the person telling the story.

Meanwhile, this is also activating what is called neural coupling. If you've ever listened to someone telling you a story and it reminded you of something else that you heard, such as a statistic or even another story, then you have experienced neural coupling. Basically, experiencing a story allows us to then connect the ideas and actions in the story to the ideas and actions that we have in our minds. So, everyone listening to the same story are all having the same regions of their brains activated, but the neural coupling is what personalizes our own response to the story. By slotting the story, we hear into our own thoughts and understanding of the world, and neural coupling allows us to better retain and appreciate the stories we hear. Listening to facts without a narrative structure activates two regions in the brain, yet the process of neural coupling allows for stories to activate many regions.

Finally, the body also releases chemicals depending on the content of the story. The most common chemical to be released is dopamine, which triggers a pleasurable feeling and one that makes a story easier to recall. A straight fact or ad copy doesn't release dopamine and therefore is harder to recall at a later date. While the effects of dopamine release may not be perceptible within consciousness, the brain itself is happier for having it released, and this creates a connection between the information in the story and a feeling of positivity. In many ways, this is the same reason your dog learns to sit when you use treats to train it. When the dog hears you say "sit" and it performs the corresponding action, it is rewarded with a treat. When our brains recall what we heard in a story, they are then rewarded with the treat of dopamine. The fact that recollection of information is improved through storytelling makes StorySelling a must in your campaigns.

But dopamine isn't the only chemical that can be produced through hearing or reading a good story. We are able to control the emotional response in our audience through our stories. If we create something with twists and turns, the audience will be on the edge of their seats. This is because the change in direction creates a sense of wanting to know what happens after. We naturally want to know what happens after in stories anyway, but when you make it hard to predict what that upcoming moment is going to be, the body reacts by producing more adrenaline. People's hearts beat a little bit faster, their breath catches in their chest, and their attention narrows its focus onto the story. You use the processes of the brain to hook them onto what you have written. Likewise, this can be used to make people feel a depth of love that is lacking in typical day-to-day activities. You can do this by writing about love, but that isn't the only way. That story about the mistreated puppy that the animal shelter wrote. If it ends with that dog being adopted into a loving family, then it is a surefire bet that the reader's mind is pumping out lots of oxytocin (the love hormone). These emotions, regardless of whether they are anticipation, love, or relief, all help readers to recollect the stories at a later date.

All of these are powerful neurological components that are triggered by storytelling. But they lead to a big question that we should consider. Just why exactly is it that storytelling is able to affect the human brain this much? For that, we need to turn our attention backward in time.

Stories: A Part of Our Biological Evolution

The reason that humanity is the dominant species on Earth is entirely due to our ability to tell stories and converse in a language. Before we had science, which can be thought of to represent data and statistics, we had story. Tribes would gather around the fireplace and tell stories of the day. In doing this, they were able to communicate dangers to each other and identify patterns. For example, if one member of the tribe got sick by touching a certain plant, then the other members would learn about this in the stories that were told that night. This would allow the tribes to carry wisdom forward into future generations to ensure that they survived to pass along their genes to their children.

Very early in human history, before the written word, we had to learn how to share these stories. They were our first form of science in many ways. David C. Lindberg touches on this in his book, The Beginnings of Western Science. Where we understand death as what happens when the human heart stops beating, early man would not accept such an answer. For early man, the reason for someone dying had to be as specific and personal as that person had been. Every death was a story. Likewise, every storm that passed wasn't a weather phenomenon but rather an angry deity. The sun didn't just rise and fall; it was pulled across the sky by a chariot. It was stories that shaped the world, not facts and statistics.

And so, it was stories that shaped the human brain as it developed throughout the ages. We know that our brain is still quite old in design. The modern era has opened up the world so that anyone can interact with anyone else, but our brains are only truly capable of maintaining about 150 social connections. This number comes from the size of the tribes of early man as the brain was developing. It is also why elements of xenophobia and racism can seem so deeply rooted. To early man, the outsider was the enemy. Those inside the tribe were connected closely to one another, but it wasn't because they shared the same blood. They were connected because they shared the same stories.

Sharing stories around the campfire was built into our evolutionary development specifically to deepen that sense of connecting with those around us. The mirroring effect was one that strengthened the tribe and kept it together because a tribe that was united was a strong tribe. When tribes found themselves falling into civil strife, both sides quite often would then perish. By mirroring the neural activity of those involved in the storytelling, the sense of community grew. Neural coupling was added to this to allow those involved to connect the stories they heard to what they experienced, and this allowed the tribe as a whole to benefit and share the learning and wisdom beyond just the initial story itself.

In many ways, our brains aren't fit for the digital age. They are most comfortable in the past. But as marketers, we can use the storytelling focus of the past to find massive success in the present. By creating stories that teach, inspire, and promote a sense of closeness between our brands and our readers (or our customers and our readers), we tap into the power of our evolutionary past and unlock the unlimited potential of StorySelling.

THE POWER OF BULLET POINTS

Building your very own sales minisites can be somewhat of a task - no uncertainty! In the wake of making an item, you need a site to offer it from, yet for some, this step has a lofty expectation to absorb information. The way toward making a sales minisite is one territory that occasionally prevents potential internet advertisers from benefitting on the web.

This step is essential; you need to profit on the web. You additionally require a sales website to attract affiliates, get engaged with joint ventures, or to give your internet promoting business any believability. It's undeniable; however, why this step causes many web showcasing learners to stop in their tracks. There are a few different ways around this sticking point.

Here are 5 top ways you can quickly use to accelerate the way toward making a first sales webpage for your internet advertising venture.

1. Use Video.

A video sale page usually has a video, a couple of visual cues, and a purchasing join. When you have shot your sales video at that point, making the page is the simple part. By utilizing video, you promptly get rid of the vast majority of the issues of web graphics, designing content, creating a sales letter, and bunches of HTML coding.

The massive advantage of including video as your sales message is that you can likewise exhibit your item directly there on the screen. This is ground-breaking advertising.

2. Use Outsourcing.

When you choose to re-appropriate your minisite creation, you will require a spending limit to pay your consultant. Fortunately, there are a great many highly talented and innovative web engineers out there who can enable you to out. Independent locales like Elance or Peopleperhour have arrangements of the individuals who can make your minisite.

On many of these independent locales, you don't have to pay anything until you are happy with the outcome. Additionally, those keen on taking your venture will show the amount they are eager to take to finish it, so they attempt to "out offer" one another. These two elements will, in general, minimize the expenses and find you an extraordinary line of work at an incredible cost.

3. Use Someone Else's Site.

If you don't have an item yet, you can utilize another person's site and sell their thing as a member. Even though this doesn't get your site ready for action, it allows you to acquire cash, gain involvement, and to fabricate your very own rundown purchasers. This likewise encourages you to learn a touch of breathing space while you get your items ready for action.

Another enormous preferred position of this procedure is that you can see the kind of sites that are changing over guests to purchasers and profits. This can give you great pointers to what you have to incorporate into your very own minisite venture.

4. Use Templates.

Templates are site page spaces. They have every one of the highlights of the finished page like features, subheads, tribute boxes, shot records, and purchasing joins, yet none of the nitty-gritty substance. This leaves you allowed to connect your data and change the template into your own sales page.

The massive bit of leeway here is that your sales page will be your own. Indeed, even-even though you began off with a standard template, your very personal data will transform it into a sales minisite that nobody else has. You can also incorporate your very own graphics, video, and so on to change it into something exceptional.

5. Use PLR Products.

Personal name rights items (or PLR for short) regularly accompany their very own sales destinations. You can ordinarily alter both the PLR item, and the sales site, thus produce an exceptional piece, yet also a remarkable sales minisite. You don't need to do this. At any rate, you should embed your purchasing join into the sales page to make the site your own.

Any of these techniques can cut off the procedure of making your very own high benefit sales minisite. You have to recall that the way toward making website pages is vital to internet promoting, however, to get ready for action you don't have to put in a long time sweating over a hot console.

The First Steps to Building A Profitable List

When you need to be effective, you should do all that you can to achieve that objective. You can't sit before your PC with no thought of what to do, complaining of not getting the benefits you want. You have to work by contributing ample opportunity, cash, and exertion if you anticipate results.

How would you begin?

You should initially pick a specialty and afterward drill down to a profitable subspecialty. This should be possible by first choosing what hobby you need to assemble your business around. This could be something you are enthusiastic about, something you are keen on, or something you need to find out additional. Try not to discount a specialty since you know nothing about it as you will learn as you research and assemble your business.

Nonetheless, don't pick a specialty since it is profitable as you will before long think that it is repetitive to assemble a business around something you have no enthusiasm at all in. You should constrain yourself to make items, compose articles, and market that business.

Then, go to Google AdWords Keyword Tool to locate a profitable subspecialty. Enter a spending limit of $10 every day. Pick the United States and Canada as your area.

Then, enter your picked specialty as a watchword. Snap on the 'More Like This' catch' Then take a gander at what different catchphrases are shown. These will be your subspecialties. Snap on the 'More Like This' Button for considerably more watchwords.

Hope to perceive how well known every watchword is. Pick one that has at any rate 10,000 indexed lists as these will be specialties individuals are keen on.

When you recognize what subspecialty, you need to manufacture your business around, you should accomplish more research to discover what issues individuals are as of now encountering and what individuals are discussing.

Do this by joining gatherings in your specialty and perusing what individuals are discussing. Take a gander at the titles of books on destinations, for example, Amazon and ClickBank. If somebody has composed a paper regarding the matter, they have done research and observed that theme to be more than likely a profitable one. Go to a few article directories and read a couple of articles in your picked specialty.

Presently make a lead magnet otherwise called a moral influence that you can giveaway at no expense to allure individuals to join your list. This lead magnet should instruct somebody yet not how to do it. Your paid item will do that!

Set up a squeeze page with a compelling headline, a sentence or two as a presentation, a few bulleted advantages found inside your lead magnet and a solid invitation to take action.

Direct people to your squeeze page utilizing either free or paid techniques.

Consistently part message everything including your headline, bulleted focuses, hues, the content on your suggestion to take action catches, illustrations, and so forth to find what performs best.

Squeeze Page Secrets of Successful Profitable Affiliate Marketers

Numerous successful affiliate marketers have been utilizing the squeeze page as their first presentation page to develop their business. This model of point of arrival works very well as it will empower you to gather the guests' subtleties, and you will have the chance to catch up with them through email. Since you will contribute a great deal of your time and exertion in driving consistent traffic back to your site, you will need to ensure that your squeeze page changes over. Here are the following segments you should know:

Part #1 - Attention Grabbing Headline

This is the first segment that your guests will see when they visit your site. You will need to ensure that you put in the most significant advantage in your feature with the goal that it will catch the guests' subtleties. When you are merely beginning, you will need to pick one great feature and track the reaction of your squeeze head. When you have a logical progression of traffic back to your site, you will need to test with another feature to attempt and improve the change. The best thing you need to do is to gather your very own rundown of feature formats so you will almost certainly use it at whatever point you need to change the feature.

Part #2 - Bullet Points

You will need to rundown down the qualities that they will get from you if they join your bulletin. This is critical as you will need to guarantee that your newsletters will take care of a portion of their issues with the goal that it will urge more guests to join your rundown. You will need to outline down in any event 3 to 5 benefits in visual cue group with the goal that they will almost certainly look rapidly and settle on the choice on whether they should join your rundown.

Part #3 - Ensure the Opt-In Form Is Above the Fold

The majority of the guests have limited capacity to focus so you will need to ensure that they will probably observe your excellent advice without looking down the site. You will need to make the selection in the procedure for your guests to be as necessary as could reasonably be expected. Do guarantee that you have put in specific sentences which will let them know precisely the things that your guests need to do to join your pamphlet.

Here are 3 of the many secrets you have to know whether you need to make a squeeze page that changes over more guests into endorsers. Do make sure to continue tweaking your squeeze page so you will get the best picks in changes.

WRITE A KILLER CALL TO ACTION

As any salesperson will tell you, you are not going to make the sale unless you ask for the order. That's why in copywriting the call to action is so important. It is the very objective of your promotional piece!

The call to action can involve a number of things, depending on what is being sold and at what stage in the selling process the promotional piece represents:

• Request more information

• Download a brochure

• Agree to see a salesperson

• View an online demonstration

• Accept a free trial

• Ask for a free estimate or quotation

• Place an order

A call to action is more than just telling the prospect what to do after.

As the copywriter—and de facto salesperson—your job is to motivate the prospect to take action. You need to inspire him or her to make the decision to fill out the form or make the call to respond to the offer.

Start with the Objective

The way you write an effective call to action is by starting with the objective. What is it, exactly, that you want the reader to do after?

For example, if you are writing a direct-mail letter promoting a new business directory, the objective of your call to action might be to get the prospect to fill out the enclosed order form and mail or fax it back. So, your call to action might be the following:

Complete and return the enclosed order form.

That's not bad. In fact, it's actually more than many promotional pieces do, some of which have no call to action at all. However, the above example isn't very motivating. What's missing? An effective call to action has these characteristics.

• It explains clearly what the reader must do to respond to the offer

• Tells the reader exactly what he or she is going to get

• It expresses, or at least implies, a major benefit

• It asks the reader to do it now, and provides a good reason why

• It says "Please"

Based on the above points, it's time to take another look at the business directory call to action:

Need a fresh crop of qualified sales leads for your business? Please complete and return the enclosed form today to activate your subscription to Endless Leads Monthly. Don't delay. The special price is due to expire Jan. 15th.

Does the above example meet the five conditions above?

• It clearly tells the reader how to respond: "…complete and return the enclosed form…"

• It describes what the reader is going to get: "…your subscription to Endless Leads Monthly…"

• What about the benefit? That's in the very first sentence: "…qualified sales leads…"

• It tells the reader to do it now ("today"), and backs this up with a good reason why: "The special price is due to expire…"

• And, of course, this call to action says "Please"

Where do you put your call to action statement? That depends on the promotion. In short pieces, like advertisements, put it at the end. In a longer promotion, such as a sales letter, it's effective to repeat the call to action more than once. However, always have one at the end.

PSYCHOLOGICALLY ADVANCED
COPYWRITING TRICKS

The term "sales and marketing psychology" may sound very technical and quite intimidating but is actually easy to understand once you get the hang of it. After all, sales and marketing psychology ultimately boils down to human nature. The trick, thus, is to use your knowledge and understanding of how people think, feel, and make decisions in pitching sales to your target buyers.

Having said that, we will be talking about how you could get inside the heard of your target buyer so as to convince them to buy whatever product or service you are offering. To do this successfully – and effortlessly, to boot – it is important for you to master the foundations of sales and marketing psychology. Here, we will talk about the 11 psychological sales triggers, the very foundation of sales and marketing psychology, so as to enable you to convince practically anyone to buy whatever you are selling.

If you are ready, let us go ahead and discuss these 11 psychological sales triggers.

Psychological Trigger #1: Fear.

Fear is one of the most basic and most innate emotions – and this holds true not only for humans but for all members of the animal kingdom. Since human beings are sentient, we feel this emotion particularly strongly. The universality, as well as the instinctive nature of fear, makes it a very powerful motivator. We see the power of fear almost every day, from electoral campaigns to health advisories. One common example of how fear is often used as a motivating factor is in the case of anti-smoking ad campaigns. In certain places, cigarette manufacturers are mandated to include a graphic warning as to the negative health effects of cigarette smoking. Anti-smoking advocates also employ a similar strategy, with anti-smoking ads showing graphic images of how long-term cigarette smoking can affect the human body. By capitalizing on fear, one can move the target audience into action.

That said, you must be careful when using fear and must only use it in the right way. One way of using fear when marketing a product or service is by amplifying a negative effect. For example, soap commercials would often place emphasis on bacteria, virus, and disease transmission. In the same vein, those selling locks would often talk about criminality and the possibility of burglary. By playing up on your target buyers' fear, you can sell your product or service in a way that would make it seem like the only viable solution.

Psychological Trigger #2: Transfer.

This concept might sound new to you, but chances are you are quite familiar with this already. This concept is not used that often in TV commercials, but it is a fairly common strategy in print ads and promotional pages of websites.

In a nutshell, the concept of transfer is hinged on social proof or transitive trust, which really is just fancy and technical speak for brand connection. To illustrate this concept better, let us say that Brand Y is a new and unheard-of product. Since it is new, people will be hesitant to try it, especially since there is no guarantee as to its quality. To overcome this hurdle, the marketers of Brand Y can namedrop familiar brands which it has collaborated with, in this case, let us say Company A and Company B. Since people know Company A and Company B, and they know that these are reputable companies, they will also associate such good reputation with Brand Y. That said, this strategy is most fitting for newer brands which can best be marketed through familiarity with other brands, seeing as consumers are more likely to patronize a product or service which is connected to something they already know or trust.

Psychological Trigger #3: Bandwagon effect.

This is among the most popular and most understood psychological sales triggers. The bandwagon effect is a phenomenon wherein people do things (or in the case of sales and marketing psychology, make purchases) because other people are doing the same. This behavior is rooted in people's psychological need to belong. Essentially, all human beings, in one way or another, desire to be a part of something regardless of whether they might realize it or not.

I am sure that you have seen how this phenomenon plays out among entrepreneurs. Whenever something becomes popular – be it a movie, a product, or even a person – you will notice a meteoric rise in related merchandise and people who sell such merchandise. Since people generally want to belong, they tend to be willing to spend on products or services which are popular among their peers. The great thing about this strategy is that it requires minimal effort on the part of the seller or marketer. Basically, people will naturally gravitate towards products or services which they view as "in" or "trendy".

Psychological Trigger #4: Comparison.

Related to the past concept is comparison. Human beings have an innate fear of standing out or missing out. Basically, we inevitably compare ourselves to our peers whether or not we may notice that we are making such comparison. This operates in two ways: first, we do not want to be the only one doing something in a particular way and second, we do not want to be the only one not doing something in a particular way. Hence, we are more likely to try something new if we see that everybody else is doing it already.

In terms of purchasing behavior, this means that consumers are more likely to try new products and services when they notice that their peers are already using these new products and services. Unlike the bandwagon effect however, which requires that the consumers themselves observe the existence of the trend in question, comparison is something that can be completely manufactured to suit the purposes of the seller or marketer. That being said, you can appeal to your target buyers by mentioning that everyone else is buying or using whatever products or services you are selling. Essentially, you want your target buyers to feel that they are missing out on a lot if they do not make a purchase.

Psychological Trigger #5: Liking.

This is another psychological sales trigger that I am sure you are well aware of. The concept behind liking is quite basic, really: if you like someone, you are more likely to do what they say. This is where the power of celebrities come in. Brands pay good money for celebrity endorsements for one simple reason: well-liked celebrities who have a large and loyal fanbase can easily drive up sales. After all, people are more likely to heed the advice of their favorite celebrities. This means that not only are fans more likely to make the same purchases as their celebrities, their means permitting, but they are also more likely to purchase products which their favorite celebrities endorse.

Hence, another infallible sales tactic is enlisting the services of a prominent individual to endorse a particular product or service. Of course, not all companies can afford to do this, in which case sponsoring a celebrity (letting a celebrity try out a new product or service for free in exchange for social media exposure) is a viable alternative. The mere association can do wonders for the product or service in question.

Psychological Trigger #6: Authority.

This concept is somewhat similar to the preceding one, liking. Whereas liking works because individuals are more likely to do what someone they like says or does, authority works because people are more likely to heed the advice of someone they respect. In a sense, authority functions as social proof, an attestation as to the credibility or effectivity of a particular product or service. That said, when a person of authority says or prescribes something, people are more likely to take an interest and to take action.

How the concept of authority plays out in sales and marketing psychology is interesting. After all, actual authority is not always necessary as the mere semblance of it typically works already. Case in point would be commercials on antibacterial soap, toothpaste, or even shampoo which features actors wearing lab gowns talking about the merits of the products being endorsed. These individuals are not really doctoring or scientists, but because they are being presented in a way that is akin to authority, the target buyers become keener to listen to them and, hence, more likely to buy whatever product they are advertising.

Psychological Trigger #7: Reciprocity.

Another powerful concept which sellers and marketers can make use of in improving their sales is reciprocity. The concept of reciprocity is quite simple. It sends to the potential buyers this particular message: if I gave you something for free, then now it is your turn to buy something. This is why whenever new food products or items are being introduced, the sellers would typically provide free samples. This is not only to convince their target buyers that their product is of high standards, but also to get them to feel compelled to make a purchase.

The concept of reciprocity is no longer only applicable to in-person sales. Quite the contrary, it works just as well for online websites, particularly those offering particular services. For example, fitness websites that earn money by selling and making workout and meal plans often provide subscribers with a free program sample. Websites which provides online seminars, meanwhile, would often give out materials absolutely for free. Even creative websites which offer a host of products such as desktop or mobile phone wallpapers will often provide some of their products to the general public for free. Giving out such samples certainly help target consumers to get an inkling as to whether or not they will actually enjoy the product or service in question. But even more importantly, by providing samples absolutely for free, no strings attached, sellers or marketers are able to create a connection between the product or service they are providing, and their target consumers. In a sense, target consumers feel somehow obligated to make a purchase, especially if they enjoyed the sample to begin with. Think about it: this strategy works perfectly fine with app and streaming services free trial, right?

Psychological Trigger #8: Commitment and consistency.

This concept can best be summarized as conditioning people to say yes but using it effectively can be a little trickier than the other concepts. Basically, your goal as a seller or marketer is to try to get people to say yes – and say yes consistently. To do this, you must remain not only committed, but also consistent. Hence, if you take a stand on an issue, then you must stick with that stand all throughout your marketing spiel. Doing so will not only lend credence to whatever product or service you are pitching but will also help your target buyers to formulate their own expectations and act in accordance to such expectations.

This brings us to the crucial question: how do you condition people to say yes? The answer is actually a lot easier than you might think. The technique is to ask seemingly innocent questions which you know your audience will always say yes to. Thus, the trick is to not ask individual-specific questions, the answer to which will vary depending on the personal tastes and circumstances of the individual. Instead, ask questions which appeal to the human experience in general. By asking questions which your target buyers can easily say yes to in the beginning, you are putting them in a mood in a position where they are more likely to agree. This increases the likelihood of them saying yes when you ask the crucial questions with regard to availing of the product or service which you are pitching.

Psychological Trigger #9: Scarcity.

Scarcity is a concept which I am sure you are quite familiar with, seeing as it is used practically universally not only in actual markets but also in online channels. The concept of scarcity operates on the basis of two things: first, limited time and second, limited supply. Limited supply is more straightforward and more in-keeping of how we understand scarcity. The lower the supply, the higher the price. And in the case of certain products or services, this low supply-high price combination further drives up the demand by virtue of exclusivity. This is especially relevant in present times when social media is everywhere, and products are more easily accessible. A lot of individuals struggle to be unique, to find products or services which could set them apart from the group. By availing of a scarce resource, individuals appear to get an edge over their peers. Time and time again, we see businessmen make use of the concept of limited supply to drive up the price of products, particularly of necessities. After all, when the demand is inelastic, consumers are willing to pay for goods or services regardless of the price thereof. At present, however, limited supply is used to sell not only necessities, but also luxury goods and other trendy, exclusive pieces. The case of Supreme, a well-known high-end street fashion brand is a great example.

Another way to use scarcity is to play up the concept of limited time. This is a typical scene in limited time offers of products and services, often at large discounts. By providing a timeline by which target consumers may avail of the product of service in question, the seller or marketer is able to convince the target consumers to buy immediately, at the risk of losing such a great deal.

Psychological Trigger #10: Dual-role persuasion.

Just because human beings are in fact emotional decision-makers does not mean that logic does not form a big part of the advertising process. After all, individuals still prefer to make emotional decisions which they can later rationalize or justify to themselves – and the same is true when it comes to purchasing behavior. That said, consumers are more amenable to spending extra if they feel that such extra spending is justifiable in light of the present circumstances.

This is where dual-role persuasion comes in. Essentially, this concept merely entails presenting both sides of the argument (albeit it must be done in such a way that you are still able to sell your side of the argument but without your biases being too obvious). By presenting both sides of the argument, you will get the appearance of being more trustworthy. After all, individuals do not like to be manipulated, so they lean away from one-sided sales pitch and towards those that gives off some semblance of fairness. In addition, by employing the double-role persuasion, you will make your target buyers feel as though they have already done their research. This works in your favor because (1) if they do not do research at all, then it means that your version of the sales pitch will be your target buyers' sole source of information with regard to the product and (2) if they do not feel manipulated into making a purchase, then they are, in fact, more likely to make such purchase.

Psychological Trigger #11: Length implies strength.

Finally, we are onto our last psychological sales trigger – length implies strength. Now, this last concept finds application in various forms of advertisements, from TV commercials to print ads, but it proves most effective when it comes to printed materials. Basically, length implies strength simply means that the sheer length, amount, or volume of proof that you have as to the effectivity of your product or service will be viewed as indicative of the strength of the said product or service. Now, we say that this is more effective for print ads than it is for other media because print is harder to consume and digest. While people might still watch or listen to commercials, and afford to be discerning, most people do not have the time to take a moment and digest long-form sales pages or read through testimonials.

That being said, including a lot of testimonials or other scientific backing to the claims of your products or services will allow your products or services to be viewed in a positive light. In a world where individuals rarely take the time to read very long text posts, the sheer length and amount of information can easily be taken as a good sign. Of course, it is better to make the content as engaging and possible, and to ensure that the claims are true, but it is worth knowing that length alone can-do wonders for your sales or marketing pitch.

As you can see, these 11 psychological sales triggers are quite common and definitely things that we encounter on a daily basis. This is especially the case now that the Internet and social media are pretty much everywhere and there are fewer and fewer people who find themselves without access to social media. This gives sellers and marketers an even greater opportunity to practice various marketing techniques and strategies, providing them with an even greater avenue through which they can practice their marketing skills.

The psychology behind sales and marketing may sound overly technical at first, but it really all boils down to having a deep understanding of human nature. These all mostly come down to human nature and our innate fears, desires, and even apprehensions. By making use of things which are inherent in all human beings, and doing so skillfully, an effective seller or marketer can successfully make their sales pitch without being annoying and unbearable. Hence, mastering these 11 basic concepts can certainly work wonders for your sales and marketing strategy. By understanding how people make decisions, you can create copy that speaks to each of these psychological triggers and actually cause people to take action on purchasing your product or service.

Chapter 12. Copywriting For Email Marketing And Direct Marketing

Among the many online activities, newsletters are still of some importance today. Email marketing is a digital marketing activity that still works, especially if integrated into a structured communication campaign. It differs in newsletters, DEM (Direct email marketing), and transactional. According to a study, 12.4 billion emails were sent via the platform in 2017, with an opening rate of + 35.7% compared to the past year. In the United States of America, over 240 million advertisements are received via email: around 7.7 for each user. 61% of these are discounts and promotions, yet I find that the most interesting information in the report concerns the reasons Americans decide to subscribe to a company newsletter:

- need for information and insights with respect to a given topic (35% of respondents)
- a reminder that is a sort of let's stay in touch (20.4%)
- interest in the proposed contents (18.4%).

But how to write a newsletter effectively? Here are useful tips:

Use an Object That Can Intrigue: A statement is often weaker than a question. In just a few words, you have to push the recipient not only to open the mail but also lose a few minutes of his life to understand what we are talking about.

Be clear: Transparency always rewards, but confusing periods or attempts at click baiting will lead the user to abandon or, worse still, get angry.

Customize Those Who Register: Customize those who register often and leave the name, and there is software that can retrieve it to insert it in the text, even in the object. The more personal the message is, the more the user will be willing to open the email.

Work at Smart Call to Action: Always give a reason to take action; it is not enough to say Buy, so to speak. The user wants to participate in the purchase process, does not like orders.

Remember the Visuals: The graphics are important. Make sure that the messages are well-integrated with the images.

Propose Exclusive Content: Doing Content Marketing does not mean obsessing over the reader with content represented to exhaustion on multiple channels. A good newsletter must offer exclusive content and always give the idea that by writing you can access an exclusive type of offer.

Most people go into copywriting in order to make money, not do the work for free in their spare time. As a freelance copywriter in particular, you need to be careful about the clients that you are looking at to make sure that you find the ones that will really work well with you and will pay you when everything is done.

There are many fantastic clients out there. They will answer your questions in a timely manner, pay you by milestones, and will fall in love with the ideas that you present to them. They pay you on time and make it pretty easy for you to enjoy your job. Unfortunately, while there are quite a few great clients that you will be able to work with, there are also a lot of bad clients who will make you want to pull out your hair and quit copywriting right away. These are the clients that procrastinate all the time, who are difficult to get ahold of, and will neglect to pay for you and just disappear when the work is done.

As a beginner, you are going to run into more of these clients than you would probably like to admit. There are always shady clients who are going to look at you and think they are able to take advantage of you. But there are a few things that you can do to watch out for those bad clients including:

- The price is too high—if you are looking at a job posting and notice that the price is really high for the work, higher than what is considered normal for the work that is requested, you should run away. These clients are usually just trying to attract beginners to do the work. The issue is that they will promise all this money but won't sign a contract and often take the work without ever offering a payment. Always be careful if the rate doesn't seem to fit in line with what is usual in the industry.

- The price is too low—most clients will list out how much they are willing to pay for the work. If you notice that the price is pretty low, it is probably not worth your time. The client will expect to get high quality work for a price that is well below market value, and you will probably waste your time. Make sure to charge a rate that you are comfortable with and stick to that.
- Won't do a contract ahead of time—it is always a good idea to get started with a new client by writing a contract. This is going to be a good way to protect you and the client. This contract is going to list all the things that will happen while you are working together, including the work to be completed, the cost, and the deadlines. If a client won't fill out the agreement, there is probably something that is going wrong, and you need to be careful.
- Clues inside the posting—sometimes you will be able to see that there are issues with the client within their posting. If the wording keeps changing, there are issues with the grammar, or something else seems off with the posting, you should proceed with caution and look for another client to work with.
- The workload changes—when you read through the job posting, you will look to see what the workload is about and then fill out your application. Sometimes though, you will spend time talking to a client, and they will try to change the scope of the work or add on a lot more and still want to pay the same price. These clients often prove to be difficult to work with and will keep changing the scope or adding on more work without paying you extra. Set out the terms right away and only do the work that was agreed to.
- Client is hard to get ahold of—if you are having trouble getting your client to answer your emails or calls and the job hasn't even been awarded yet, you may need to worry. Times

get busy, but if your client goes days without talking to you and then all of a sudden show up again, you are probably dealing with a difficult client. Give them some time to respond, but if it seems to take too long, it may be best to pick someone else to work with.

Learning when to spot a bad client is one of the best things that you can do for your career. There are a ton of clients who are excellent, pay well, and are a joy to work with, and you will find plenty of these along your journey. But you will find that one bad client can ruin it all for you. So, make sure you are looking for some of these signs each time that you apply for a new job and find out which clients are the best for you.

Post comments on other related board pins, especially bigger sites with 1000 plus followers.

Remember to include the most important points for your audience and topic and to be helpful and knowledgeable at the same time.

Facebook Checklist

Purpose

To build social reach and attract new likes/followers from other sources. Use Facebook to find existing and new customers to share experiences with using media to give a multi-dimensional snapshot of what you offer.

Policy

Create interactive content that engages new clients through multimedia with use of popular #hashtags.

Procedure

Research popular trending travel related #hashtag topics, find other websites using these and like, contribute to, and comment on their pages. Offer content to big sites who want quality images and content to post. Comment on their content.

Look for topics your clients are interested in and create connective content between your site and theirs. Contribute to these pages with positive comments, interacting with potential client audiences.

Include #tags in content on your pages and other sites for your travel niches and on external Facebook pages.

These should be used EXTENSIVELY on bigger Facebook pages you have previously liked.

Consider adding Facebook or blog comments to blogs.

Add:

- Images – good quality pictures and videos
- Add # hashtags
- Add URL where appropriate
- Comment on other posts
- Contribute to other peoples' pages with helpful, relevant content

LinkedIn Checklist

Purpose

To create a visible presence on Linkedin

Policy

Stay

Procedure

Follow topics that are being explained and leading personalities in the field you are writing content about. Engage with content and people.

Add:

•Images – good quality pictures and videos

•Create and contribute to discussions that are relevant to your audience

•Add URL where appropriate

•Comment on other posts/discussions and add useful ideas and contributions

•Endorse and invite other members

Use statements including phrases like:

•How to

•Why people

•You could

•If you

•Ways to

•Top reasons to

•Tops reasons why

•Why it's

•Things to consider

•Important things to remember

With all social media, remember to include the most important points for your audience and topic and to be helpful and knowledgeable.

There are two important starting points to remember when implementing your Google+ strategy:

First, use keyword and intent based combinations of phrases in your Titles and...

Second, use very specific and correct formatting of your posts' content. If linking to a page, use a sufficient number of words to make the post highly relevant to the page your post points to. If not linking to a page and creating an image post, make sure the description is a decent length to make it more searchable in Google+ and generic search engines.

Google+ Checklist

There are four steps you need to walk through when implementing any Google plus strategy:

1. Keyword and target page research and layout

2. Acquiring RELEVANT Followers

3. Participating in communities and commenting on posts (building relationships)

4. Posting sequence and formatting for Google search to make it easy for your audience to find your posts/page

Ensure that your Google+ posts:

•Are extremely targeted to the right audience (use keywords from your main website page titles)

•Are engaging and encourage curiosity (talk about the reader and what they want, then tie the features and benefits of your products and services into your post copy)

•Contain the right blend and number of #hashtags (4 to 5 maxima per post)

•Contain the right number of keywords (300 words - fewer is better)

•Link to the page I want to teach Google to have high relevance to my audience (to improve my overall website authority and relevance)

•Motivate readers to take a desired action or learn more by inserting copy that builds interest and trust (ask them to do something other than buying, e.g., read more about [insert what they are interested in in the form of a feature or benefit]

•Position you as an authority in your niche to both Google and visitors

•Help Google serve up your content as often as possible

•Lead visitors to a landing page that delivers what you promise in your content. This is the first step in your sales funnel (yes, your offsite content IS part of your sales funnel). Using templates dramatically reduces the time needed to post awesome posts both Google+ and your audience will love.

Policy

There are some steps you need to walk through when implementing any Google+ strategy

- Keyword and target page research and layout
- Acquiring RELEVANT Followers
- Participating in communities and commenting on posts (building relationships)
- Posting sequence and formatting for Google search and making it easy for your audience to find your posts/page
- Using specific keyword phrases in your Titles and...
- Using specific and correct formatting of your posts content – using text that is copy rich but sounds natural and non salesy

Procedure

Ensure consistency across posts, so they are...

Extremely targeted to the right audience

Are engaging and encourage curiosity

Contain up to 7 #hashtags

Use descriptions: a minimum of three descriptive paragraphs

Use *Title* around titles to tell Google the title should be bolded and that it is the post title

Link to the page you want to teach Google to have high relevance to your audience (to improve overall website authority and relevance)

Motivate readers to take a desired action or learn more by inserting copy that builds interest and trust

Position you as an authority in your niche to both Google and visitors

Help Google serve up your content as often as possible by making it super relevant to popular keyword phrases

Using templates dramatically reduces the time needed to write awesome posts both Google and your audience will love.

Contain "hooks" to relate your content to your audience's interests and desires. Relate their needs and wants to what you have to offer, deliver value to prospects, and lead them to a desired action as part of your sales funnel. And yes, your offsite content IS part of your sales funnel!

Add hashtags you want to use. Use up to 5 hashtags and include some that relate to the main generic topic, plus some that interlink (meaning that they are placed on many closely related posts you have written). Make sure your hashtags are highly relevant to what the post is about. This reinforces your credibility and means any hashtags that get clicked will bring up posts that are only of interest to readers and won't turn them off.

Plan out your posts. One in 4 to 5 posts should be about a product or service you promote. The rest should be interesting, helpful or informative to readers. Give them something of value in each post, such as a post that teaches them something even if it's small.

The job of non-product and service promotion posts is to educate the reader so when you do promote posts about "your stuff", you don't have to try to throw all the features and benefits into a commercial looking post.

Write 5 posts leading up to the "sales post" that talks about the benefits of linseed oil for shoe leather, how to choose the right color polish for your shoes, about the foundation of shoe polish, and some funny stats about how many shoes the average puppy eats before becoming a grown up dog.

Entertain your audience while TEACHING them that you are the expert, and that there is a long thought out process or history behind your product or service.

Think about this as you construct your descriptions, and use our who, what, why, where, when, how, question worksheets to help you come up with some engaging ideas for posts.

When you are posting to Google+, here are the golden rules:

Use appropriate hashtags.

Descriptions are to be a specific amount of words long except for gallery pics. You can use page content as a base for descriptions but change some text, so they are unique.

Post to public circles 3 to 5 times a day and once a week to a big community.

Once a week, pick a popular post that has been posted on a community page then share that post with another community and/or your own page. Pick posts with lots of engagement.

Comment on one to two posts per day on other profiles and communities.

Join communities and follow Google plus pages that are relevant to your page.

PROMOTING YOUR CONTENT

Social media, linking, ads, email.... these are all ways you can promote your page.

Again, work on quality not quantity. Think relevance not numbers! Semantic search wants to see connections to and with your page by relevant sources.

When you create content for social media or any other promotional material, here are some guidelines to follow:

Make the content you post highly relevant to the article/page you are sending visitors to. Create a mini version of the article using similar keywords and hashtags. Use images that relate to your page as well.

When encouraging likes and shares, comment on similar posts that have been posted by authoritative sites. You want as many people as possible who are known as authorities to acknowledge your post. This is especially important for Google+ (which I love, as it helps Google find and index your page faster).

Create bios as a third-party description of yourself and add an enticing call to action within it.

ESSENTIAL COPYWRITING
TECHNIQUES TO USE DAILY

According to a study, a person receives on average 121 copies a day. There are 121 different messages, 121 different promotions, 121 different call-to-actions.

With all these copies, yours can easily get lost in the recipient's inbox, another way. How can you distinguish yourself by pointing out your copy? Or rather, how can you make the recipient read it and interact with its content?

This is where your copywriting techniques come into play. The way you structure and compose your copy can greatly affect your click-through rate (CTR). From the words used to personalization, the content of the copy is as important as the object.

Below are some copywriting techniques you can use to improve the results of your campaigns.

Improve the CTRs of Your Copies Thanks to These Copywriting Techniques

Use the PAS formula

When you learned to write in elementary school, you were probably taught to compose a theme. The theme was to have an introduction, a body, and a conclusion. You had a model or formula available to put together a well-written essay or letter. Fortunately, there is also a good copywriting formula for copies. This is the PAS formula; PAS is an acronym which stands for:

P: Problem

A: Shake

S: Solve

•Problem

Problem is the phase in which you identify the problem of the reader. What are they doing to solve the problem? And why is this a critical point to explain the question, you can paint an almost real picture of the problem. So real that it can evoke emotion during reading.

Why does it work?

Because the emotion is directly connected to the problem. People do not try something new or take a different path unless they are tired of not getting the desired result. By painting this almost real image, readers are emotionally involved with what they say. From here, you begin to establish a relationship of trust. Trust is the key factor that allows you to convert these moderately interested readers to very interesting ones

•Shake

Agitate, literally agitation, is the phase in which a bit of salt is figuratively thrown on the problem's wound. At this stage, you will indicate other reasons why the problem must be solved. Perhaps the problem is related to the lost ROI? A lack of organization? Deadlines not met. Whatever the intrinsic reason, you will highlight it to evoke other emotions.

But don't throw too much salt on the wound. You don't have to upset your readers. You want them to be frustrated, but still interested in solving the problem.

•Solve

And now the fun part: the last part of the copy is where you can do everything the best. At this stage, you will share the solution to the problem.

After reading and identifying with the emotions you mentioned earlier, your readers are more likely to try to solve the problem (and act!) Because they are ready to find the solution. They believe you understand them, and you know exactly how to help them.

Take Advantage of Bucket Brigades

The brigade buckets are simple words or sentences with the colon at the end. They are very effective in convincing people to continue reading your copy.

The bucket brigades ignite the interest of your readers when they are about to lose everything. They are a way to involve them again without forcing the hand.

Here is the list of proven bucket brigades:

- Things are like this:

- Now:

- The conclusion is:

- You are wondering:

- Absurd:

- It's not over here:

- But here's the twist:

- The best part?

Feel free to use proven options in your next copy or create your own.

Simplify

When it comes to copywriting, better not to overdo it. This is absolutely why it is called copywriting.

Depending on the type of copy you are sending, the actual copy may be long (with the need to scroll) or short (without scrolling). Both types are fine. However, the words used to compose the copy must be words that are absolutely necessary for the copy to make sense. In essence, you want to get rid of the superfluous.

Here's how:

•Make your message clear: your copy will certainly have a purpose. In order to achieve the goal (or to allow readers to take the necessary steps to achieve the goal), they must understand your message. If you use too many words, the message can be lost. If you use too few words, they will not understand what you are saying at all. You must use the right amount of text to explain your purpose without being too verbose.

•Take advantage of peer review: asking someone to review your copy is not only positive in terms of grammar, punctuation, and spelling but also ensures that your copy makes sense and is effective. It is also a good idea to have different people see different copies: in this way, the same person does not get used to your writing, as they can no longer identify if something is wrong. Today it's very easy to find freelance writers able to review your copies, and you can use, for example, Fiverr, Upwork, and other freelance platforms.

•Outline your content: think about the information you want to include before you start your copywriting. In this way, you will be facilitated in the composition of the copy, but you will also be certain of the fact that the content is aligned with the general objective. While choosing content, ask yourself:

- Is it suitable for the purpose of the copy?

- Do the readers need to know this? If so, why?

Customize your text

When you receive or read a copy, it's nice if you are called by name or the body of the copy is designed specifically for you. Do you feel special, or not?

Well, why not adopt the same technique in your copies?

Taking the time to personalize your text can have extraordinary and positive effects on both CTR and your revenues. One of the easiest ways to customize copies is to use the reader's or recipient's name at the beginning.

The body offers another possibility of personalization. The content obviously depends on your products and services, but ultimately, it should be exclusive to the reader.

In this case, you are customizing the copy with the items actually purchased, and you are also able to provide advice on complementary products.

Use a PS at the end

Remember when you received letters from your friends who always put a PS in the end? Your eyes surely always went there before reading the actual letter.

The same effect occurs when you use them in your marketing copies.

A PS is a good way to strengthen the point of your copy. Whether you are promoting a discount, an added value or a new product, your readers will surely notice the PS and only then will they read the actual content of your copy.

Some things to keep in mind regarding PS:

•Don't use them anyhow: use them only when you have something specific and important that you want to highlight. Excessive use will have the effect of making them confuse with other contents.

•Include a link: the links in the PS segment can generate more clicks than other segment of your copy. Make sure it is relevant and worth the click.

•Do not worry: your PS must be short and direct. If it is too long, the message can get lost in a thousand words.

Start Improving the CTR of Your Copy

The copywriting is not on the way to sunset. They still represent one of the best channels for engaging and converting potential customers into real customers.

By making small changes to the copy, you can increase CTR and overall ROI. But don't make all the changes together. Try one thing at a time so you can see what works and what doesn't.

EASY COPYWRITING FORMULAS
THAT CONVERT

With the advent of technology and the growing connectivity in the modern world, it is not at all surprising to find that effective copywriting has become an even more valuable skill. With so many avenues that can be used for advertising and marketing, business owners are all too willing to pay copywriters hefty amounts in exchange for good copy. But what if you are a business owner who owns a startup company? What if your startup business is still not earning enough for you to outsource such an important task to a professional?

Well, the simple solution to your problem is to just do the copywriting yourself. That is only commonsensical, right? However, this leads to another problem, that is, what if you have never written a copy before? What if you do not really consider yourself that much of a writer?

Fortunately for you, while copywriting is indeed a skill that requires practice to master, understanding its basic principles is not really rocket science. In fact, there are a couple of super easy, tried and tested formulas which you can use in writing your ad copy. As long as you know what these formulas are, you already are in the running towards writing great ad copy.

In this chapter, we will talk about two copywriting formulas that have proven to be effective and successful. Even better, these formulas are really easy to use. All you really have to do is to plug in the information about the product or service you are offering, and you are pretty much done. Of course, it will take some practice to fully master this copywriting formulas. While practicing, however, you can refer to these formulas every so often.

So, if you are ready to learn how you can write your copy in a way that will translate to sales, let us jump right into the first copywriting formula.

Easy Copywriting Formula 1: Problem, Agitate, Solution

The first copywriting solution that we will discuss is what is commonly referred to as the PAS pattern. PAS stands for problem, agitate, solution. The good thing about this formula is that you can use and apply it anywhere and everywhere. All you have to do is insert the details pertaining to the product or service you are selling, marketing, or advertising and you should be good to go.

Considering the flexibility of the PAS pattern, you can use it in writing copy for your sales page, Facebook advertisements, email ads, and even video sales script. Just note, however, that there is greater involvement when it comes to video sales scripts, so that one might take a little more practice.

The PAS formula is extremely effective because it allows the seller, marketer, or advertiser to get people to naturally want the solution being offered. Since the target consumers do not feel like a particular product or service is being pushed down their throats, they are less likely to object to the solution being introduced. That being said, this copywriting formula heavily relies on well-known concepts in sales and marketing psychology. It is highly effective because human beings are conditioned and predisposed to move away from pain and move towards pleasure.

Given all that, we now go to the meat of this section: how does one use the PAS formula? Simple. One just has to follow the following simple steps:

1.PROBLEM. Tell your target audience about the problem they are facing.

2.AGITATE. Remind your target audience of all the reasons why the said problem is causing them pain. Amplify the problem by making it seem more significant or more difficult than it actually is.

3.SOLUTION. Present the solution to their problem which, in this case, is using the product or service you are offering.

To understand this formula better, let us take an example. Say you are selling a frizz-taming hair product. So, how do you use the PAS pattern to convert your target buyers to actual buyers?

First, talk about the problem. Since you are selling a frizz-taming hair product, you can start by saying something along the lines of "One of the most common hair problems people face during humid weather is frizzy hair." Now, you can make that statement as formal or as informal as possible depending on the style and tone you are going for in your copy, but that is the general principle.

Second, agitate the problem. Not only do you want to remind your target buyers of the problem, but you also want them to really feel inconvenienced by the same. You can thus follow up your first statement with "Dealing with frizzy hair can really be a pain during busy mornings/ Having untamed hair can make you look unprofessional/Frizzy hair can keep you from making a great first impression." Try to make this part specifically tailored to your target buyers.

Finally, present the solution. Remember that your goal here is to sell your product, so after amplifying the problem, you also have to present the solution. This is where the usual marketing pitch of "This frizz-taming hair product will help keep your hair looking sleek no matter the weather." Since you have amplified the problem, your target consumer will likely be more receptive to the solutions you will be offering.

Easy Copywriting Formula 2: Desire/Hook, Solution

Despite the simplicity and effectivity of the PAS formula, there are instances when the same is not always the most appropriate copywriting formula to use. Sure, the PAS formula is fitting for longer copy, but if you do not have that much of ad space to work with, then you need a formula that will serve your purposes better.

This is where the Desire/Hook-Solution formula comes in. Compared to the PAS formula, the Desire/Hook-Solution formula allows for greater flexibility. However, it is also a formula that requires more practice than its counterpart. The beauty of this formula, however, is that it gets the point across quite quickly. This makes it incredibly effective for smaller ads where you have to catch the attention of your target buyers right away.

Before you can practice working with this formula, however, you must first understand its basic tenets. There are two steps you should follow which are:

1.DESIRE/HOOK. In this step, your goal is to immediately grab the attention of your target audience. You can do this by using a powerful statement or by starting off with a statement as to what your target audience desires.

2.SOLUTION. Immediately after getting the attention of your target audience, you present them with a solution right away.

This formula involves only two steps, thereby making each step even more important. To make sure that you will be using it the right way, let us go into a deeper discussion of each of the steps. For this purpose, we will be using the same frizz-taming hair product for our illustrative example.

For the first step, you really want to start off strong. This is where creativity and a way with words really come in. You want to reel in your target consumers, and you can only do so by delivering a powerful statement right off the bat. Going back to our previous example, you can start off your copy with "Want to get shiny, sleek hair fit for a goddess?" Notice how vivid the imagery is? It is just one sentence, but it paints a picture in the minds of your target audience right away. It evokes emotion, stirs desire, and arouses curiosity. This will make your target audience want to know more about the topic.

For the second and last step, you will now be presenting the solution. Note that at this juncture, your target audience is already curious and interested. They have already taken the time to stop whatever they are doing in order to find out more about the statement you have just mind. Thus, all that is left for you to do is to show them how they can get the results or solution they want to desire. That said, you can thus follow up your first statement with "Then use this frizz-taming hair product to get a great hair day every day." Notice how this second statement is straightforward? With the advent of the Internet, the attention span of people has greatly decreased, so you do not want to waste their time with a long-winded pitch. Instead, you just want to deliver the point across right away while they are still interested.

Copywriting can be quite intimidating, especially if you have no prior experience in the area. With practice and the right copywriting formulas, however, you should do just fine in terms of writing great copy. The two copywriting formulas above are tried-and-tested, as well as very easy to use. All you have to do is plug in the details of the product or service you are selling, and you already have a great copy in your hands. Plus, the more you practice, the more naturally will these formulas come to you.

Mistakes to Avoid

We looked at the strategies that successful companies employ to sell their products better. In this one, we will look at the mistakes that you must avoid while preparing copies. It is important to understand that mere rights will not suffice, and you must be able to avoid the mistakes, which might show your company and products in bad light.

Features and benefits

When copywriters create copies, they tend to mention the benefits and forget to add the features of the product or service. Both are equally important, and the customer should be given a sense of all that there is on offer.

If the features are not mentioned, then it will seem like the company is trying to hide something or a particular feature is not available. It will also look like the ad has been done in hurry and half- heartedly. So, it is best to list out every detail of the features or at least the majority of it.

Bad layout

A bad layout will not just cause the product to not sell itself but also cause the company to look bad. This is especially true for a company that has already made a name for itself. The layout must be neat and clean and there should not be any out of place elements. There should also not be too many words being repeated.

Most copywriters are also quite creative, and they will know exactly where what needs to be places, but to eliminate any bad layout, it is best for the editor to check it before sending it out.

Some of the things to bear in mind when creating an ideal layout include the following:

- •Making use of a catchy and effective headline
- •Using numbers instead of spelling them, example- saying 10 and not ten
- •Avoiding using number lists. Bullet lists are more preferred

- •Most sentences should not be any more than 3 or 4 sentences long and these sentences should be short or medium in length
- •The various headers you use before a paragraph need to be apt and something that the reader wants to read
- •The headers should clearly state the content of the paragraph and not be misleading
- •When it comes to SEO writing, you must make use of all the appropriate words to make sure that they allow the ad to appear as the first result on popular search engines

Bad language

Bad language can kill a copy. This point was mentioned in the positive strategies and is being repeated here because it is extremely important to have good language. There should be an aesthetic appeal to the words and sentences being used. If there are too many adjectives, then it will start to look like the company is trying too hard to sell a product.

The language must be clean, comprehensive and effective. There should also be no use of difficult words and jargons, which might make it difficult for the customer to understand the ad or worse, misunderstand it.

Irrelevant pictures/ media

Many times, there may be wrong pictures or irrelevant pictures being added into the copy. These might have been added by another department, who might not know what is being stressed on. That might cause the ad to look bad and so, it is best for the writer to check the ad before it is sent out. It will also be key to use the exact pictures of the product and not generic ones. The customer might be disappointed to get a product that is not similar to the one shown in the pictures and might even return it for the same reason.

Too many distractions

There should be not too many distractions on the page, especially if they are portraying unnecessary things. In fact, unnecessary things must not even be included in the copy, no matter what the circumstances. These might be gaudy pictures or big words that don't have any relevance to the copy. If there are certain design elements such as speech bubbles being used, then they must be placed aesthetically, such that they don't interfere in the text. They should also be kept small and preferably placed in the corners of the page.

Trying too hard

When making a copy, the information should be given out in a subtle manner. There should be no begging in the copy to make people buy the product or service. Appearing desperate might cause people to be repulsed and your products and services might not be accepted. It is important to know how much information to give away and how much need to be curtailed.

Depending on the stage at which the product is, the copy must be designed. If the product is new, then as much information needs to be given out. But if it is old, then it should be presented with the new features that it incorporates. Information should not be repeated, and the copy must not contain lots of information.

Not trying at all

The point being said, it should not be too subtle either and not convince people to buy the product. If the customer senses that the copy has been made carelessly, then he will judge the product or service as having the same quality. That will make the product look bad, even if it is not the case. So, there should be just the right amount of information that should be provided in the copy and it is best to look at a competitor's copy to get the right idea to create the copy for your product or service.

Bad headlines

Several copywriters make a mistake while preparing the headlines. The headlines are supposed to be intriguing and not passable. At the same time, it should not be overtly informative and over intriguing. It will only cause the customer to dismiss it off. The right headline must contain the right words and a short sentence, which will effectively drive the point home.

There should be no jargon, as it will cause the customer to move away from it owing to not being able to understand it. Many times, in a bid to appear unique and not sound common, the copy writer might make the mistake of putting up a very headline to make it eye catching. But that might backfire, and the headline might create a problem. Making it excessively witty or humorous might also cause a problem, as the customer might not take a liking to the approach.

Wrong tone

The tone of the copy should be chosen depending on the product and service. It should not come across as being casually written and also should not appear too serious. If there is humor to be added, then it should not be too generous.

It should be the right blend of key words and good grammar. The tone should also not be offensive, just to be able to garner attention. It will backfire and not serve the purpose it was meant to. There is certain etiquette to be followed when it comes to creating a copy. It is important to follow the guidelines and the basic layout of copy writing, which includes maintaining the right tone.

Not being covered legally

One mistake that copywriters might make is, use controversial material and not be covered legally to take on a public litigation. Some of the words that should not be used or used sparingly include – no risk, guaranteed results, 100% money back etc.

If these are true, then they can be added sparingly and not made the headlines. And if these are not true, then you can add them and add in a disclaimer to either tell the truth or that certain conditions apply.

THE SECRETS TO COPYWRITING SUCCESS

When you do start your own business, you should make sure that you maintain a good relationship with all your clients in each project. You can do this by meeting all the objectives of the advertising campaigns on a regular basis and maintaining a professional relationship with all your clients. You should deal with project challenges professionally. Some of your satisfied clients may send some business your way in the future if they are pleased with your work.

Qualities of a Successful Copywriter

If you are wondering if you can do this for a living, read the following qualities of most successful copywriters to see if you have what it takes:

You need to read about your product

The products that you will be selling are meant to make people's lives easier. You have to convince them that they need it now. To do this, you need to learn about the specifications of the product and what separates them from similar products in the market. You can't just write about something that you don't know about. People will buy what you are selling them if you sound like you know what you are talking about.

Gadgets are one of the most popular types of items online. Successful gadgets have specific characteristics that make them better than others. If you are selling a smartphone for instance, you should know about the screen size, its camera's megapixels, its available colors, its manufacturer, and its operating system. If there are too many types of information to cover, you should put yourself in the buyers' shoes and think about the information that they want to learn before they decide to buy the product. The information you learn will help you create an effective copy.

You need to keep learning

A copywriter is a combination of a professional advertising engineer and a salesman. As technology and society change, so do the needs of the people. There are copywriting tricks in the 70's that are still useful today. On the other hand, there are important copywriting tricks today that will no longer be effective tomorrow.

Right now, you are learning the basic principles of selling through your writing. If you want to become a copywriter, you should continue to keep up with the online advertising trends. You should continue to look for strategies and tips that may improve your copywriting abilities. Your experience and your ability to learn will help you beat your competitors in writing effective sales copies.

You need to know the right price for your service

If you successfully find clients as a freelance copywriter, you need to know how much to ask for your services. Copywriters are an essential part of companies that sell products and services. Your copies will bring money to the company. If your clients return to hire you in new advertising campaigns, you should know when to increase your asking price for your services. If you are good enough, clients will be happy to increase your pay.

You need to know how to adjust based on your target market

If you work hard and become a professional copywriter, you will need to sell different types of products and services based on the clients who hire you. To cope with the needs of different types of companies, you need to learn how to talk to different types of people through your writing. You don't need to be a great English writer or a litera-ture major. In fact, almost all copywriters these days write in a conversational manner.

You should understand that you are not writing for any other purpose other than to sell the product. However, directly telling someone to buy something is not a good sales strategy. Your job is to create a desire, a need and a sense of urgency in the reader. You need them to act. This is what your clients expect from the copies that you create.

You need to have a want to succeed

Copywriting is not for everyone. Some people are contented with a 9 to 5 job. If you are one these people, copywriting is not for you. However, if you really want to be financially successful, copywriting is a great career path to take.

You can only be a successful copywriter if your copies can sell tons of the target products. Everybody had their own bad experiences about sales. Everybody tried to sell something at one point in their lives. Everybody experienced the pain of being rejected. The quality that separates the successful seller from the unsuccessful ones is their ability to continue selling even in the face of frustrations. Moving on from failure is easier with copywriting because you are not facing the people you are selling to. Your drive to become successful will help you forget about your frustrations and continue writing copies that sell.

Your task as a copywriter

A copywriter's task is not just to create emails and ads. It is more than that. A copywriter's job is more than just selling goods and services. A copywriter solves problems. As a copywriter, you are helping your readers with a specific problem and you are convincing them that their problems can be solved using the product that you are promoting. You can do this by understanding your readers. Here are some readers' characteristics that you need to consider when writing a copy:

People hate salesmen

People hate it when a salesman is trying to sell them something. It doesn't matter if the product is the best in the world. Hard selling sales tactics do not leave a customer feeling good. As copywriters, we want our readers to feel good when they read your copies.

People enjoy buying

People love to make a purchase. They like the feeling of buying something new or making life easier with a new service subscription. However, they also want the feeling of control when they buy something. They buy things based on their emotions towards those items, but they want to be convinced that there is a good logical reason behind the purchase. Your readers hate the feeling of losing money for something worthless.

People avoid traps

If your message sounds like a sales pitch, people will think that it is a trap. They will think that the product you are offering is not worth the money. They may think that it is overpriced or below their standards. A badly written copy will sound like a trap that will take away the readers' money and not provide them with the service or product that they expect. Your aim is to write a copy that sounds natural. It should not sound like an ad from TV shopping networks.

IMPORTANT QUESTIONS TO ASK
BEFORE YOU HIRE A COPYWRITER

Anybody can claim to be a copywriter as we have learned after numerous trials and tribulations, regardless of whether it's in the physical business or whether your business is on the web. Anybody with the information of the language and who believe that they are imaginative progressed toward becoming copywriters. In any case, brace yourself for what I'm about to tell you. It is quite difficult.

There is a lot of cash and business to be lost if you place your ad campaign in the hands of juvenile, the individuals who claim to be copywriters, however, are exceptionally somewhat more than unreliable administrators.

That was at that point, presently, we have discovered that there are a few components to compose a good ad campaign. This must be additionally pushed. Notwithstanding if you do sub contact your ad campaigns, there are specific questions that you should ask your copywriter.

Trust me, and it will spare you from a great deal of head throb, assets, and money that is legitimately yours. Besides you get good ad campaign that would produce income for you.

You should find attractive solutions to the questions that you posture to the copywriter, whom you mean to utilize.

In case the person neglects to answer the questions, isn't eager to answer or the answers are not sufficient, at that point well you ought not to utilize the person.

When utilizing the copywriter

Search for honesty and trustworthiness in the answers. If the person isn't coming clean, they will slip someplace. Search for their experience and request their qualification Do a historical verification and converse with the referrals that they have mentioned.

Copywriters are good at making trust in what they state, after all, that is the thing that they are getting paid for. That is why I have developed a lot of 12 questions, which can disclose to you whether you need to enlist the person or not.

1. What are you are as of late written ad campaigns - direct mail advertisement/web pages/TV and radio ad jingles for the objective shoppers -

The answer to the question will reveal to you whether they are appropriate for the job or not. Copywriters are an accomplished part and some arrangement in specialty markets. In this manner, pick the person who has already written for the specialty advertise that you are going for.

2. If it's not too much trouble appear at any rate three instances of your practical work

When the copywriter posts you the work, you would know whether they have worked expertly, or they are merely beginning. If they have answered yes to the main question, then they would have no issues in explaining and demonstrating to you their work.

In case their answer is negative, at that point, you realize that they are novices who are merely beginning and need to make an ad campaign learning at work. They may make botches for which you may need to pay.

3. Give your reference (ought to exclude family, relatives and the individuals who work under and with you)

This question is intended to give foundation data and check to their work. When they provide references, the current utilized can check whether what they have expressed is truth or they are talking plain lies. It's effortless to discover. Accordingly, copywriters give their references all around cautiously. They give of those whom they trust will provide useful input to their present business

4. Is this an all-day job for you?

By answering this question, the copywriter will tell you what they accomplish professionally. If they work all day job elsewhere, by what method will they have the option to commit the time, for your campaign? When you can find that there is a copywriter whose full-time occupation is that of copywriting, you have met your match.

5. What is your experience?

The experience that the copywriter gives you ought to be sequentially written if they have ever worked for an ad office as a copywriter, at that point that is an advantage for your campaigns. In case they have never worked as a copywriter, at that point, hiring this person can arrive you in a difficult situation.

6. Have you written a copy for the web site; do you have your very own web site?

In case you are searching for web copy, at that point this person ought to be for you. If they have a website, the following question ought to be whether they have written their copy for the website or they have depended on outside assistance. This is fundamental in case you are searching for a copy that is web related. Survey the work and the website of the copywriter to realize whether that is the sort of yield you need from the copywriter or not.

7. What is the average time of finish for the undertaking?

A practical and good copywriter can't produce work medium-term. This question tests the gauge and the work timetable of the copywriter, regardless of whether they have enough work and how bustling they are. While asking this, you can check whether they can adhere to their conveyance plans.

8. Okay, subcontract the work, or would you do it without anyone else's help?

The answer to this question will let you know who is going to take the necessary steps for you. Since you will be paying for the job, you reserve a privilege to know. If they are sub reaching the work, it may be to a person who has lesser aptitudes and experience, and they are out to procure a snappy buck.

9. In what structure will the work be delivered to me?

We usually like the work to be delivered in full that is organized with two-three alternatives, which ought to be accessible. Since we would prefer not to spend more money on arranging, altering, and so forth, this sets aside personal time and cash, and we get an item, which is ready to be delivered.

10. What amount would you charge from me?

Since you would pay, you should realize the amount they charge, what might be the installment plan. Will they bill every hour or every day and so on compensation when you are entirely fulfilled about the job that you have given them?

11. If the copy that you compose doesn't work, what might be likely explanations behind it?

Typically, a good copywriter would know the business sectors, customers, items, and administrations well. This is the motivation behind why they would likewise give you recommendations to make the copy beneficial. They will tell you the advantages and the impediments of the copy. Along these lines, the answer to this question is incredibly significant for you.

12. It is safe to say that you are set up to be paid on a commission basis?

By and large, the answer will be a "NO." In any case, if most sales rep work on a commission basis, at that point, why not a copywriter, if they have confidence in their capacity, then they ought to proceed with the commission strategy. After all, they are additionally in the business of selling, the selling of good campaigns which consequently will get the incomes and the benefits for you.

At first, it tends to be a downtime installment. When you fabricate an association with the salesmen, the installment can be made based on commission.

Find the solutions before you procure them.

Significantly, you get the privilege and the right answers before you approach hiring the copywriter that you need.

It can mean a difference between a campaign and an extraordinary campaign.

The campaign where will get you the income or will do your business or shut your shop.

CONCLUSION

Now imagine that you can dedicate your brand to copywriting. To radically change your days, investing your time in the production of marketing materials, without this being an obstacle anymore because copywriting will be easy and natural for you.

Imagine your office full of packages ready to massacre customers, sales letter, newsletter, imagine your blog full of articles, and then your book ready, finished, with a beautiful cover.

When it comes to building your brand, it can be easy to get a little too self-promotional. This is where copywriting on your site can make a big difference.

There is not much to add, and this profession attracts the attention of those who love to create and would like to write for work. There is a lot of attention around copywriting.

I'll tell you right away: there is no defined path in the sense that there are no degree courses or professional registers. There is only, on the part of those who want to undertake this activity, a great love for creativity and writing that you've learned from this book. That's enough?

Hence, to become a copywriter, you must read. In fact, you need to study and study the theory. It is not enough to love writing; you must know the basics and the rules. But it is necessary to focus on the persuasive copywriting techniques and on the pillars of communication you are exposed to in this beautiful copy.

The journey of learning and improving is never-ending…and I hope that this book gave you some help in your business and if so, I would be the happiest person in the world.

www.ingramcontent.com/pod-product-compliance
Lightning Source LLC
Chambersburg PA
CBHW071720210326
41597CB00017B/2545